My Watermill Story

by Jill Fraser

SARGANT PUBLISHING

First published in 2009 by Sargant Publishing
2 Tower Lane, Aldeburgh, Suffolk, IP15 5LN
Tel: 01728 454171
e-mail: james.sargant@btinternet.com

My Watermill Story © Jill Fraser 2009

A catalogue record for this book is available from the British Library.

Sargant Publishing would like to thank the photographers for their kind permission to reproduce the images in this book. Every effort has been made tor trace and contact the photographers and copyright holders.

ISBN: 978-0-9563792-0-7

Cover images by Laurence Burns and Charley Sargant

Printed in Great Britain by CPI Antony Rowe, Chippenham

MY WATERMILL STORY

Contents

Two sets of plates can be found between pages 32 and 33, and pages 96 and 97

Preface

This is very much Jill's Watermill story written as time permitted between 2002 and 2005 with two intensive periods in 2005 – one outside the chalet at the top of Trudie Willis' beautiful Suffolk garden just outside Aldeburgh and the other in the idyllic setting of the garden of Valerie Solti's villa on the coast in Tuscany on our last holiday. It concentrates on her twenty-four plus years as Artistic and Executive Director of the Watermill and her particular memories, feelings and opinions. If she had had the time, she might have written more about the first years of the Watermill, but a lot of what she has included has been gleaned from letters, documentation and conversations, in particular with Judy Gollins, from whom we bought the freehold, rather than from careful and studied research.

Little, if anything, is included of events and productions after that last holiday and her death in February 2006 when the chronology ends, although she was still working hard on the completion of the 2006/07 season and her plans were well under way for what was to have been her last season before the freehold of the property passed to the Trust and a new Artistic and Executive Director was in place. She was working for much of the Wednesday, which ended in her going into hospital with a chronic pneumonia. She had attended the press night of Jonathan Munby's highly successful production of *Tartuffe* on the Monday night in company with Rosie Hoare, one of her very greatest friends and a contemporary of Jill's on the Stage Management course of the Central School of Speech and Drama in the sixties. She died just two days later on Friday 10th February.

That it has taken so long to get to the point of publishing this small book was really determined by doing my best to fulfil what would have been Jill's first and foremost wish, being to ensure the future of the Watermill as a theatre and that it should be handed over in 2008 in a healthy state, both artistically and financially. This has been achieved with the artistic help of John Doyle and Edward Hall and I must not forget the third Associate Director, Euan Smith, a constant figure around the Watermill throughout our time at the theatre. The appeal for £3 million launched in 2005 has reached its target and the Trust, Hedda Beeby, its new Artistic and Executive Director and the theatre's ever loyal staff are taking the theatre onwards and upwards – they are indeed 'flying'.

My particular thanks to Ade Morris for his 'Final Chapter', to James Hogan and his team at Oberon Books for helping to make the publication possible, to Samantha Preston for her patient picture research and to Clare Lindsay, who has been part of so much of our Watermill years. Not forgetting Sam and Charley, who have been bullying me to 'get on with it'. Jill would be just so proud to know that, in the end, they are both pursuing the same sort of careers as we both did.

James Sargant 2009

Any profits made from the sale of this book will be donated to Breast Cancer Care (Charity number: 1017658)

Prologue

In 1981 James and I bought the Watermill Theatre from its former owner Judy Gollins. A tiny, picturesque, converted watermill in the heart of the Berkshire countryside, over one hundred and eighty years old and surrounded by the mill wheels, beams and rusting cogs of its former incarnations.

Not the sort of thing you ask advice about before doing, for the simple reason that any rational person would have said it was foolhardy. Foolhardy maybe in terms of financial investment – in those days no-one would have dreamt that such a theatre building could ever have any real worth as a going concern, but for two people who had worked all their lives in theatre – a dream come true! To have your own theatre, to be able to work with directors and designers, actors and musicians, producers and stage managers on plays that you yourself had chosen. To be part of a programme of work for the local community – to share with everyone your passion for live theatre. What an incredible opportunity!

It has been a fantastic journey of twenty plus years. There have been constant battles to keep the theatre financially afloat and times when the energy and optimism almost gave up, but miraculously we have survived – no, more than that – we have flourished and proved to the sceptics that, with commitment and passion for what you believe in, you can succeed beyond your wildest dreams.

The one thing there has never been time for is writing the memoirs. People ask constantly about how the theatre started and I have always promised myself that I would find the time to sit quietly and capture some of the special memories to intersperse with the facts about how the Watermill was born. Well, the years go by and the shows keep coming and that time never seemed to materialise! However, four years ago something happened to make me get on with it.

My life began to change slowly but surely in March 2001 when I was recalled to the breast screening headquarters after I had had a routine mammogram at the mobile unit in Tesco's car park. A few days later a letter arrived assuring me it was just a routine check, but the results had been unclear – nothing to worry about, but could I confirm an appointment for later that week? If there was nothing to worry about, why the hurry? Anyway, I played the game and told myself that it probably was just routine, I couldn't feel a lump and I felt well, maybe it was just a faulty machine…but it wasn't…the radiographer told me that they had found a small lump and showed it to me on the monitor. They needed to do some tests to find out whether it really was cancerous, but the likelihood was that it would be. It was a devastating moment. My life flashed before me…my family's future that I wouldn't be part of…everything that I had planned for the theatre that now wouldn't happen…then a wonderful nurse swept me up and took me to a private room, gave me a cup of tea and told me that it wasn't the end of the world – it was a small lump and they could operate. She went on to point out that we only read about the bad statistics in the press and we never hear about all those people who recovered from breast cancer. Things moved fast after that and I found myself in hospital within ten days having a lumpectomy – a week later I was back in again, as they hadn't removed enough. There followed weeks of infection and draining, which was restricting and tiring, but I was able to carry on working fairly normal hours. I found the best way of dealing with the whole situation was to carry on as normally as possible. I didn't take more than a few days off work. I eventually had five weeks of radiotherapy five months later. Regular tablets for the rest of my life and regular check-ups for the following five years were prescribed. I was more than relieved when I was told in February 2002 that I had the all clear.

If I thought being told that I had breast cancer was devastating, nothing really prepared me for the moment five months later when my body started to ache and my ribs cracked. I was told I had secondary breast cancer in the bones. This explained the cracked ribs and the aching body. Was there a cure? To me the word 'secondary' meant a death sentence. My oncologist and my GP were frank. There was no cure, but the progress of the cancer could be halted and it was possible for it to go into complete remission. This was again followed by the reassurance that we only read the bad news in the press, we don't hear about all those people who live for years, having kept cancer under control. A change in medication and monthly injections to strengthen the bones was the way forward – after six months a decision would be made as to whether radio or chemotherapy would be needed.

I had to do something positive myself too. I read lots of books about cancer causes and cancer cures and, having looked into several extreme diets, I gradually worked out a diet for myself, which I felt suited me and my family's lifestyle. I eat lots of fruit and veg – organic whenever possible. Fruit juices, raw vegetables, no dairy products and no red meat. Flax seed, flax seed oil, cold pressed extra virgin olive oil, potato flour, corn pasta, soya milk are all now staple store cupboard ingredients. James, who has taken over almost all the cooking, has become a dab hand at converting recipes to use allowed ingredients! Treatment will continue as the cancer goes through different phases, but I am fortunate in having a job with which I can continue and a wonderful team around me, who run the theatre on a day to day basis. But most of all a husband, now retired, without whom I would be lost.

It is a daily battle – much as you try, you never stop thinking about it and wondering what that new ache and pain might mean. Concern for the future – and how long that will be, is always there. But there are good things too – for instance I pace myself better – I allow myself to delegate, I have lost weight – a battle I have waged all my life – and I try not to put off things until tomorrow, if they can be done today.

It is essential to have a positive attitude, to aim to be the one who confounds all medical expectations and this attitude is boosted enormously by the family and friends behind me, who are supporting me every inch of the way.

It is for them more than anyone that I have now started to write this story about the Watermill, to share with everyone the privilege it has been to live and work here.

Chapter One

My very first memory of the Watermill was setting eyes on it on a late afternoon on a perfect summer's day. James had visited previously with friends some years before and only he might have guessed, as we drove through the gate and into this magical place, that this would be more than just a social evening with David Gollins, son of the owner. David, with his mother Judy, was responsible for much of the Watermill's conversion into a theatre and some great artistic output in the late sixties and seventies.

The way there on that summer's day, with the trees beside the lane down to Bagnor, created a magical canopy of leaves through which the dappled sun pushed its rays. This was the old lane before the bypass, a lane now replaced by a raw new road...but still remaining at the end of this road, as the trees close in again, is the feeling we had all those years ago of entering a secret civilisation, guarded by the two bridges that span the crystal-clear, sparkling water of the River Lambourn. The river meanders beside the road fronted by charming sleepy cottages down to the third and final bridge, and then the reed-fringed drive into the grounds of the Watermill itself.

When you live somewhere it's all too easy to forget your first impressions and take a place for granted. The Watermill doesn't let you do that. Its utter tranquility, when audiences and actors have long retired; the trees which surround and embrace the garden; the river, which never sleeps, but rushes urgently through the mill on its never-ending journey; the echoes of a previous life in the milling stones and ancient machinery that lie around the place; all this makes it a unique spot, fed by the energy of centuries. It is a privilege to have been able to care for this extraordinary place, just a moment in time.

And as for the theatre itself, for James and myself, who had worked in numerous theatres all over the world, it had a lot to live up to, but there was no doubt that it surpassed even the finest, in its intimacy, its huge potential, and welcoming ambience. First the almost fossilised early nineteenth century iron water wheel, its wooden paddles long since rotted away, and the mill race at the entrance to the auditorium. Once inside, the apparent simplicity of the conversion adds to its charm. In the warmest sense, it has a rustic, Heath Robinson appeal. Three of the original massive solid beams that stretched the width of the building, and would have supported the huge weight of the French mill stones on the first floor, were literally sawn through to create the well of the auditorium, the saw marks on the beams can still be seen. What a heart-stopping moment that must have been! Would the structure survive such drastic surgery! Thankfully for us all it did and remains standing to this day! These mills had to be solid to house a massive weight of machinery and withstand the vibrations from the milling and the turning water wheel, two hundred theatregoers and their loudest applause will barely stir the ghosts of those days...

The show we enjoyed that August night was a production of *Tishoo* directed by the then Artistic Director, Michael Elwyn.

After the performance we joined David Gollins for dinner in the beautiful nineteenth-century tithe barn restaurant and enjoyed local trout served by one of the many colourful local characters, the indefatigable housekeeper and queen of all gossip, 'Mrs B'. We would soon get to know and utterly depend on Mrs B during our first few months at the Watermill a year and a half later. When she so sadly died a few years later we planted what has grown into a splendid Magnolia Grandiflora in her memory.

David's mother, Judy, grasping a glass of red wine, joined us as we had coffee. Not one to mince words, she came straight to the point. 'Well, do you want it?' I had no idea that this was even on the cards, so it came as a huge surprise. I then discovered that, after James's first visit eighteen months previously, he had tracked down David, a Staff Producer at English National Opera, where James had been Technical Director. They had lunch together and talked about the practicalities of running an organisation like the Watermill and David had asked him whether he would like to buy it and take over! At that time James had no desire to run a theatre, we weren't married and he didn't feel it was a task for a single person. The answer then was a definite 'No, thank you!'

Now, however, things were very different. It seemed like an incredible, once in a lifetime opportunity and somewhat inevitably we left loaded with annual accounts and reports to help us to try and fathom out how on earth the place worked. I remember travelling home in silence, both of us knowing that there was really no decision to make, by hook or by crook the Watermill would be ours and we would make it work.

At that time we had a pub called The Peacock in Chelsworth, a tiny village in Suffolk, where we went at weekends – me from my job as Administrator for the Cambridge Theatre Company and James now from the Barbican Theatre, part of his long association with the RSC. Chelsworth was a friendly, small community, which was hard to turn our backs on, but by selling The Peacock and our flat in London, as well as mortgaging ourselves up to the hilt, we were able to take on the Watermill. It was mad, but it was the right, the only thing to do!

Chapter Two

There is a mention of a mill at Bagnor in the Doomsday Book and, though records over the centuries are somewhat incomplete and haphazard, we have built up a good picture of the life of the mill over the centuries. This includes the building being a 'tucking and fulling' mill, a 'paper' mill and latterly a 'corn' mill. An elderly gentleman, who came to the theatre a few years ago, remembered it working as a corn mill in the 1920s, but by the time the Gollins family bought the property in the mid-'50s it had lain empty and disused for many years and was in danger of dereliction.

Before she died, Judy Gollins sent me a copy of a long letter she had written to a friend, describing how the theatre came into being. The letter is a free, libellous mix of fact and gossip, throwing some light on the wonderfully eccentric way in which the Watermill Theatre was created.

The Gollins family bought the property in the late 1950s for £3,000 – sadly Frank and Judy Gollins soon parted and there was a time when their neighbour at Bagnor Manor, Billy Wallace (one-time escort of Princess Margaret), almost bought the watermill that was adjacent to his land, offering Frank Gollins £11,000 for the tumbledown property. A quirk of fate meant that this deal was never finalised and Judy eventually acquired it for herself and her children.

David, the eldest son of the family of four, a student at the Royal College of Music, was passionate about classical music and his dream was to turn the mill into a cathedral, which would house the church organ he has acquired and provide a space for classical music concerts and small operas. However, conceding that the building was 'architecturally unsuitable' for this purpose, he set about making a theatre. His father was an architect and, although separated from Judy, advised David by the exchange of letters and in fact never saw the Watermill he had helped to create until long after Judy had left and James and I were ensconced.

As a full-time student, David only had the time at weekends and holidays, but with the help of his family and friends he gradually cleared the mill and burned all the rubbish, which had built up in it for years. He and his team of helpers re-pointed the bricks, re-hung the doors, so that they opened outwards to conform to licensing regulations – a discovery when the Council got involved, as no planning permission for change of use had been secured! They created the auditorium; constructed stairs; built the side galleries and turned the corn bins in the roof into dressing rooms. Judy estimated that this cost in total about £800! They had created a sort of Elizabethan courtyard theatre with an apron stage and side galleries. The best seats, which were thought to be the front row of the circle, were priced at 30s (£1.50). Downstairs they were priced at a guinea (£1.05) and 15s (75p). There were just 115 seats – reject chairs donated, fittingly enough, by Winchester Cathedral.

On September 11th 1965, the Berkshire Shakespeare Players opened the theatre with a performance of *The Taming of the Shrew*, followed by the Unicorn Opera Group presenting *La Finta Giardiniera*. These productions, and the conversion of the building, were both a resounding success and the Watermill Theatre took its first tentative steps. The sense of occasion in those days was sustained by an extended interval, when liquid and other refreshments were served by a massive log fire in the adjacent barn, accompanied by an organ recital on David's re-sited church organ. The log fire is still there of course, but the organ decamped again to be stored in the barn at the house in Boxford, where David lived in later years. I believe it is still there in pieces.

At this time the present car park was an orchard, there were no floodlights and at dusk paraffin lanterns were lit at strategic points. There were no toilets – the ladies used one in the house and the men the Elsan in the tool shed or the river!

The following year, 1966, an extended season was planned and once again The Berkshire Shakespeare Players came up with another resounding success – *Twelfth Night*. The rest of the season welcomed Progress Theatre's production of *A Man for All Seasons*, a concert of electronic music by Delta Plus and Handel's romantic opera, *Poro*, performed by the Unicorn Opera Group.

David's dream had been realised. He planned for the future to attract university and amateur and semi-professional groups and for the place to stay 'modest and informal'. Above all he wanted it to retain the charm of a family affair.

It was not, however, to be all quite so idyllic. In 1967, Peter Webster, a former actor turned producer, director, playwright and local caterer persuaded Judy Gollins to let him run a professional summer season. She charged him no rent, but simply asked that he should pay for the electricity and the telephone. It was a disaster. Equity, the actors' trade union, intervened when it was discovered that the company wages couldn't be guaranteed. Peter Webster disappeared and the season closed after only six weeks.

But lessons were learned and in 1968 David and Judy co-managed the enterprise themselves with the help of the actor, Basil Lord, who lived up the valley, and Lord Olivier became patron. The whole family weighed in to make the season a success. The eldest daughter, Jennifer, was a reluctant unpaid secretary; her sister, Joanna, became stage manager; Edward, the younger son, worked behind the bar; and David was administrator. All the actors lived in 'dormitories' in the Mill House, girls in one, boys in the other and the artistic director, David Rayner, lived in what was called 'Box 13' – a defunct horse trailer! In 1969 an investment of £7,000 was made and a soundproof lighting box, flip up seats, new curtains, heating and a mini fly tower were installed. The stables were also converted into accommodation for the actors. However, more seats were urgently needed to boost the income from attendances. Without increasing the capacity David predicted that the theatre would have to close. An application made to Newbury District Council to increase the seating from 115 to 170 was met with huge opposition. Late night parties had disturbed the then mostly agricultural community and the Chairman of the local Speen Parish Council at that time declared that the council 'consider the development of this theatre unsuitable for a small rural hamlet and the restaurant would be better provided for within the confines of Newbury or Thatcham'! They feared that the extra seats would bring too many extra cars and, with a restaurant licence until midnight, late night traffic would be unacceptable to the villagers.

Fortunately, for the future of the Watermill, it became apparent that, as a listed building, the application had to go to the Planning Committee of Berkshire County Council and they overruled local objections after they had received assurances about tree and shrub planting proposals and car parking spaces. The theatre was granted permission for the extra seats and a licence to operate for four months of the year.

The way was now clear for substantial alterations to be made, for which the then huge sum of £20,000 was borrowed: five more rows of seating were added to the rear of the circle to get the numbers up to 170; the foyer was constructed; the bar was added to the side of the restaurant; the bungalow beside the bar was built, as were the restaurant kitchen, the cloakrooms adjacent to the car park and the flat above. All this was completed by the start of the season in 1972 and, structurally, this was The Watermill Theatre we took over when on October 21st 1981 we moved in.

Chapter Three

But it wasn't as straightforward a move as it might have been. In fact we lived in the best 'squat' in Berkshire until the end of January 1982 when we officially took over the ownership. Judy's solicitors discovered a last-minute hitch – literally last-minute – our solicitors phoned James, as he sat in an almost empty London flat waiting for the final removal van to be loaded, and said 'on no account move!' While at the same time Judy's solicitors were telephoning her and saying 'on no account let them in!' Too late, I was already there with half of the first van unloaded. It transpired that in the dim and distant past, in return for the loan of £20,000, made to do the 1972 improvements, a first refusal to purchase the property had been given, if Judy ever decided to sell! There was little James or I could do, it was down to the solicitors to sort it all out, and we opted to carry on moving in, hoping that everything would eventually be sorted, as thankfully it was after an unsettling first Winter.

The whole place was in need of complete redecoration. One room in the actors' cottage hadn't earned the nickname 'the black hole' without just cause! I had never seen such huge plates of fungi growing inside a house, let alone inside someone's bedroom, and when the wind blew snow built up inside through the gaps in the brickwork! We had just three weeks to make the place habitable before actors and stage management were due to move in and start work, as we had already decided that we were going to present a family Christmas show.

There were two huge pluses to our first weeks at the Watermill. We would never have coped without the indefatigable energy, knowledge and enthusiasm of our friend and Production Manager, Clare Lindsay, who took on anything and everything, moving in with us from day one; and another dear friend, Wendy Toye, director and choreographer, who, when she learned that James and I had bought the Watermill, insisted that she be allowed to direct our first show – *The Gingerbread Man* by David Wood. We were thrilled that someone of her reputation – more at home on the stages of Sadler's Wells and the London Coliseum – should give us her support in that way. She went on to direct a show virtually every year for the next fifteen years until ill-health forced her retirement. Clare Lindsay is again alongside us as the theatre's General Manager, after a wide-ranging freelance career, and even two years as the Watermill's Restaurant Manager.

What a Christmas that was! Snow fell like it would never stop. On the morning of our first performance – a sold out show – I remember standing in our car park at 11.00 am when the show was due to start, praying for someone to arrive. Then a school rang to ask whether it was worthwhile their continuing to struggle to get to us... Yes, we cried! And half an hour later three coaches arrived – we had our first precious audience, an audience who, by their excitement and enthusiasm for the show, reaffirmed to us just why we wanted to make theatre.

Christmas shows continue to be really special events. There is nothing quite as thrilling as an audience of young people experiencing the magic of theatre for the first time. And the Watermill, in its intimacy, is perfect for letting actors tell a story and weave a spell as though it is being done just for you and you alone. Sometimes it can be overwhelming. We always know when the Wicked Witch or the Evil Wizard is really working by the number of tiny children sitting in the foyer within the first five minutes of a show! Usually they pluck up sufficient courage to creep back into their seats, clutching a parent's hand so tight as to stop the circulation! One of my favourite Christmas moments was at the start of a performance of *Pinocchio*. Jiminy Cricket made his first appearance sitting on a trapeze that was lowered slowly into sight. He was green all over – a green bowler hat, green waistcoat and tailcoat, green tights and make-up with lots of glitter. There was just one spotlight on him and a mirror ball created dancing stars all around him. A little boy, who couldn't have been more than five, was sitting in the back row of the stalls and turned to his mother with his eyes wide with wonder and gasped at her 'It's Jesus Christ!' The magic of theatre!

On the first Saturday morning of that first Christmas I remember looking at the front of the theatre and thinking with relief that the snow was beginning to thaw, as there was water running down from the eaves above the emergency exit. Slow realisation dawned however, and we grabbed the keys to the theatre to discover the stage and auditorium inches deep in water – a pipe had burst in the roof and water was pouring through the auditorium ceiling like rain. Not able to switch on the electricity until our roving electrician, Barry Spiller, arrived, we worked by torchlight to find the burst – helped by Dougie Cook, our characterful handyman, who we had inherited from the Gollins. Barry Spiller is still our electrician and is affectionately known as 'The Prince of Darkness!'

One thing we were learning fast was that, as the theatre had developed bit by bit, gradually having things added to it over the years as funds became available, there was no real logic as to the whereabouts of essential services such as the main fuse boxes or stopcocks... The stop cock to the theatre was eventually found, oddly, in a corner of the auditorium itself – and we were able to commence bailing out. With a performance due to start at 2 o'clock we had to work fast! At that time a temporary awning was constructed between the theatre and the bar to provide shelter for the audience. Unfortunately things conspired against us even more and the whole flimsy thing then collapsed under the increasing weight of the snow. Getting shovels from the workshop to clear the snow, we were met by yet more floods and burst pipes at the rear of the building – it was a miracle that we were able to welcome an audience for the matinee!

Burst pipes became the norm that winter – none of them were lagged and consequently the extreme weather had a field day. We only missed one performance however, and that was because one of the actors had gone home to Essex for the weekend and couldn't get back. We even tried to get the local RAF station to scramble a helicopter to fetch him, which, incredibly, they would have done if the weather hadn't worsened – but constant blizzards prevented even the RAF from taking off.

In spite of all the traumas we kept smiling and the audiences kept rolling up. What we hadn't anticipated was that there was insufficient electricity coming into the property to deal with all the heating up at full as well as the sudden drain of theatre lights. Lawrence Doyle, our current Production Manager, would say that things haven't changed! Although we have considerably more electricity on tap today than we had then, as productions have become more sophisticated, we still don't have enough and are in fact in the process of getting an extra supply brought into the property. Back in 1981/2 virtually every performance over Christmas was punctuated at some point by a fuse blowing. If we were in the office in the house during the daytime, pounding feet heading for the intake room at the rear of the kitchen would herald a power failure. In those days we didn't have any generator back up, so, using the emergency lights only – which automatically came on – and lots of torches, which were always on standby, the cast would stop the show and get the audience to sing carols until such time as the fuse was replaced. This also involved turning the heating off everywhere except in the theatre, so that the show could continue. Audiences were wonderfully understanding and all the rest of us just shivered – the British Dunkirk spirit always came to the fore!

It was Christmas 1990 during a production of *Toad of Toad Hall* that a great friend, Biddy Hayward, came to our rescue when there was a major all-day power failure in the whole Newbury area. She magicked a generator from a local farmer, who had recently invested in a new one. It was duly installed and the matinee went ahead. This old generator was our emergency standby for years until the Friends of the Watermill raised the funds to purchase a slightly more sophisticated version, which has proved a godsend ever since. No longer do the torches of stage managers play on the faces of anxious actors as they struggle valiantly on in semi-darkness!

There is just one more memory from that first winter that deserves telling. The company from the then London production of *The Sound of Music* had excitedly booked the restaurant for their Christmas lunch on their day off – a Sunday. We'd enlisted the help of another good friend, Andrea Leeman, to help us with the restaurant and she was due to be with us to cook a traditional Christmas lunch for the party of fifty, who were due at midday. Needless to say snow fell heavily and Andrea called at the crack of dawn to say she was completely snowed in and couldn't possibly get to us. We were on our own! Having just dealt with a routine burst pipe in one of the spare bedrooms in the house, we set off for the restaurant to start preparing the lunch. Clare, James, myself and another good friend and experienced costume supervisor, Carrie Baylis. We opened the door to the bar and restaurant only to be met by yet another huge flood. A pipe behind the bar had burst and there was freezing water everywhere! However by now we were old hands at dealing with emergencies and the long held Watermill tradition of achieving minor miracles was established. We had already invested in lots of space heaters in order to cut down on the use of electricity, so we put these on at full blast and got the log fire roaring away in the restaurant. By the time the coach arrived on the dot of twelve, you would barely have known that there had been a problem. We served delicious roast turkey with all the trimmings and were well into dessert and coffee before… the power cut hit! The restaurant was fortunately mainly lit by candlelight in those days and the cooking was complete, so it was not too much of a problem, in fact it rather added to the atmosphere of the occasion. My abiding memory of that afternoon is of all the company and ourselves sitting round the fire by the Christmas tree with June Bronhill, a soprano doyenne of opera and musical theatre and Mother Superior in *The Sound of Music*, leading everyone in a wonderful sing-along of carols and selections from other musicals. However, the day still almost ended in disaster when the coach got stuck in the car park as they tried to head home. It took a lot of strategically placed skid pads and cardboard to create a track for it to be able to finally move off. We were exhausted but triumphant, looking forward to en evening in front of the television by the fire, but it was then we remembered the power failure – not our fault this time for once, as all the heavy snow had brought down the power lines in the village. So it was early to bed.

Chapter Four

Looking back over the years, events that have happened, people that we have worked with, productions that we have helped to create, we know that we have been mighty fortunate. To be in a position to enable theatre to happen; for it to be in a beautiful part of the country; to have all the advantages of living in the country, yet with the stimulus of a city through the constant flow of creative artists year by year coming to work with you, is pretty special. Everyone who is engaged for a production lives at the Watermill or nearby, so that it is like living in an ever-changing commune but with everyone focused on a single purpose – to make theatre. The fact that everyone lives and works together for an intensive period of time produces, on the whole, good work through concentration and the minimum of distraction. There is not a lot to do in Bagnor of an evening, apart from going to the theatre or the pub and socialising together!

So many wonderful characters have contributed to the Watermill's uniqueness. Ben Pendred, an old friend of the Gollins family, was a sitting tenant in part of the actors' accommodation when we moved in. He had helped in all areas of the organisation before we arrived, working in the box office for a bottle of gin a week as payment, and for us he was an indefatigable seller of raffle tickets virtually every night of the week. The sight of Ben, in his suit, with his distinguished white hair and beard was well known to all our audience and he and his comrade in arms Billy Galloway raised considerable sums for the theatre in this way. He was also a diligent distributor of brochures and leaflets. He would set off in his yellow and cream VW van to villages all over Berkshire, Oxfordshire and Wiltshire, where he was a familiar figure in the local hostelries. His death at the age of eighty-four was a sad loss to the theatre. Margot Needham, who has sadly also recently died, was another unique personality. She worked in the box office for us prior to computerisation until we realised that she didn't really understand about decimal points and would put them where she randomly thought they should go! Many an hour was spent sorting out Margot's accounts. However, she was a diligent first secretary to the newly formed Friends of the Watermill and also created the 200 Club, which still contributes a regular £1,000 to the theatre's fundraising each year. She and her husband Derek were constant loyal advocates for the theatre wherever they went. They also then lived in an exquisite house full of marvelous furniture and bric à brac, which often found its way onto the Watermill stage, and, of course, for years Margot would invite the entire cast and production team of every show round for a splendid supper as a matter of delicious tradition. Colin Waters, who we had inherited as the Watermill's groundsman, helped to create the familiar landscape of the Watermill we so enjoy today and, when he left to follow a love to Ireland, Margot's son Duncan Mack continued the good work for many years.

In our early years the theatre was only permitted to open for twenty-three weeks a year. This was the result of the planning restrictions enforced when the hamlet was predominantly a farming community. To increase the number of playing weeks had to be one of our main targets, as box office income was after all our major source of funds. Also, and perhaps most importantly, having short seasons meant that staff had to be laid off and, if not for the often extraordinary loyalty of our staff, we risked losing really good people in the restaurant and the theatre year after year.

We are often asked what have been our favourite productions – an impossible question to answer. Each one at the time is special, part of a journey of discovery, a search for what the theatre stands for, what we are trying to achieve. From the start we were determined that it would be a theatre for all. That's why our first family Christmas show was so important for us, bringing really young children and coach loads of schoolchildren to the Watermill – giving them their first taste of live theatre. It was important to us that there should be a mix of ages and society. The Watermill was not to be just a place for a fun night out with a gin and tonic on the lawn – a poor man's theatrical Glyndebourne. It has so much more to offer and indeed we had its reputation on which to build and expand. In the very early years David Gollins' choice of plays ranged from Strindberg to Lawrence to Ibsen, as well as lighter comedies. Decisions about what a season would consist of needed to take account of a myriad of tastes within the community. It is interesting to look back and trace how we altered the balance for a while to perhaps a more broadly popular programme, introducing musicals on a regular basis and Shakespeare, dabbling with contemporary comedy, searching for the key to what would be the artistic foundation for the future. I believe we have over the last few years finally settled into a style and content, which is very recognisably 'Watermill'. We've done this by putting the directors much closer to the decision-making process. I now, on the whole, work much more closely with a small group of directors, who have talents in particular areas, and I create a programme of work using their particular skills within a broad artistic vision that I set in motion. Has it made the work substantially better? In some cases yes, but when I look back on the early years, we still produced some cracking good productions in the early '80s and '90s, many of which live on in the memory.

A magical production of *Twelfth Night*, directed by Euan Smith, was our first professional Shakespeare and featured Frank Thornton as a wonderfully melancholic Malvolio. Twenty years later Frank now comes regularly as an audience member to our Ed Hall/Propeller Shakespeare. Our second Shakespeare, again directed by Euan, was *Romeo and Juliet*. Beautifully designed by a young Scottish designer, Greg Smith. It was set on a flight of steps, which eventually became the lovers' tomb, surrounded by mummified bodies wrapped in white cloth, which were draped around the balcony. Kathryn Hunter, of Theatre de Complicite note, newly emerged from drama school, gave us a stunning Juliet with a young Sean Bean appearing in his first professional role as Tybalt. Wendy Toye's production of *This Thing Called Love*, a compilation by David Kernan and John Moffat of love poetry and songs, was our first London transfer, playing at the Duchess Theatre for a short season. This was followed the next year by the British premiere of *Snoopy, the Musical*, which also moved to the Duchess, with Suzie Blake, Mark Hadfield and Teddy Kempner among the cast.

One of the most important aspects of our work developed during the early '80s. We needed some

The interior of the theatre circa early 1960.
Photo: R Carpenter Turner.

The Interior of the theatre 1997.
Photo: Colin Willoughby.

David, Joanna and Judy Gollins with dog, 'Ugo' and
'Coquette' – circa 1963.

David Gollins.

Judy Gollins.

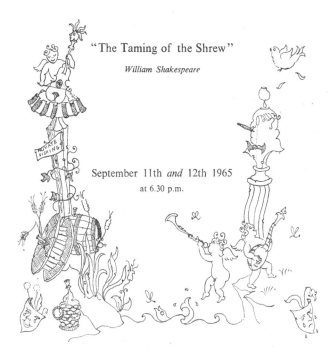

Watermill Theatre

"The Taming of the Shrew"

William Shakespeare

September 11th *and* 12th 1965
at 6.30 p.m.

Cover of the programme for the first production by the
Berkshire Shakespeare Players.

GINGERBREAD MAN (1981)
Nigel Hughes (The Gingerbread Man) with Jenny Galloway
(The Old Bag).
Photo: Frazer Ashford.

PINOCCHIO (1984)
L to R: Iain Rattray (Gapetto), Anthony Best (Pinocchio), Mark
Eldridge (Jiminy Cricket).
Photo: Laurence Burns.

SNOOPY (1983)
Lto R: Mark Hadfield (Linus), Susie Blake (Sally Brown), Nicky
Croydon (Peppermint Patty), Robert Locke (Charlie Brown).
Photo: Laurence Burns.

SNOOPY (1998)
L to R: Lewis Rae (Charlie Brown), Sally Ann Triplett (Lucy), Gavin
Lee (Linis), Lindsey Dawson (Sally), Jenna Russell (Peppermint Patty),
background: Stephen Matthews (Snoopy).
Photo: Laurence Burns.

TWELFTH NIGHT (1982)
Frank Thornton (Malvolio).
Photo: Laurence Burns.

ROMEO & JULIET (1983)
L to R: David Moylan (Mercutio), Sean Bean (Tybalt).
Photo: Laurence Burns.

BUGSY MALONE (1987)
The first production by the Watermill Youth Theatre
(The Water Rats).
Photo: Glenn Collett.

FLYING (1998)
Watermill Youth Theatre.
Photo: Philip Tull.

The Watermill ducks.

Anthony Drewe and George Stiles (1990).
Photo: Peter Bloodworth.

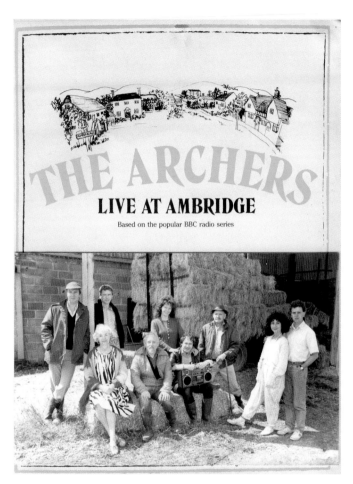

THE ARCHERS (1985)
L to R: Charles Collingwood (Brian Aldridge), Patricia Greene (Jill
Archer), Alan Devereux (Sid Perks), Norman Painting (Phil Archer),
Fiona Mathieson (Clarrie Grundy), Trevor Harrison (Eddie Grundy),
Norman Jones (Jack Woolley), Alison Dowling (Elizabeth Archer),
David Parfitt (Nigel Pargetter).
Photo: The Mail on Sunday.

HENRY V (1997)
Alexis Daniel (The Dauphin) on Eve and Assistant Stage Manager
Kellie Clare.
Photo: Laurence Burns.

HENRY V (1998)
Tony Bell (Governor
of Harfleur)
addresses Henry
V (Alexis Daniel)
and Propeller, (the
English army) from
the 'walls' of the city.
Photo:
Laurence Burns.

The Boxford Masques 2000 – *THE WELL IN THE WOOD*
Photo: Philip Tull.

THE GONDOLIERS (2001)
Josephine Baird (Bianca) and Mike Afford (Carlo Cacciattoro)
Photo: Laurence Burns.

The Summer Fair
L to R: James Sargant, Jenny Galloway, Jill Fraser, Euan Smith with
Sam and Charley Sargant.

The Summer Fair
L to R: Gay Smith, Sir Michael Hordern, Peter Murray

children to take part in a Christmas show by Christopher Lillicrap and Jeanette Ranger, *Christmas Cat and the Pudding Pirates*. Peter Murray was our musical director for the show and he ran group workshop auditions to find eight young pirate 'ratlings'. These auditions were a huge success, even with those who were not chosen, and several parents approached us to ask whether we would consider starting regular Saturday morning theatre workshops. Thus the Watermill Youth Theatre was born. At that time they were known as Water Rats, who were twelve to eighteen year-olds, and the younger Ratlings, who were six to eleven. Peter was a great inspiration and progressed from a first production of *Bugsy Malone* – the splurge guns made for that show were hired out for many years – to several he wrote himself. One I particularly remember was *Wind Among the Pines*, a story about life on the canals. I think I remember that one in particular because we hired a horse-drawn barge and took the Water Rats on a trip down the local Kennet and Avon canal to experience it at first hand. We achieved just one minute of complete silence with the kids, so that they could imagine what it used to be like, just the sound of the horse and the gentle lapping of water against the boat. Peter stayed with us for many years, forming a partnership with Euan Smith, together writing six superb Christmas shows, all with original music: *The Rose and the Ring*, *Pinocchio*, *King Rollo's Stolen Christmas*, *King Rollo Space Invader* and *Jack and the Beanstalk*, laying the foundations of the Watermill's enduring reputation for high quality, unusual Christmas shows.

As for the youth theatre, we now have over 100 young people involved with our Junior and Senior Youth Theatre and the older group, now known as The

Young Company, some of whom go on to train and work in professional theatre, in particular Jo Millson, who is enjoying a most successful career in theatre and television. Too many young people to mention have found their professional feet in the theatre through the Watermill's work experience and youth theatre. Under subsequent Directors Trev Wright, Ade Morris, Ben Myers, Will Wollen and of course Patricia Williams with the Junior Youth Theatre, the work of the groups has expanded beyond all compare, now encompassing new writing for and with young people on a major scale – from five to twenty-five year-olds. We are very proud of our young people here at the Watermill, they and their parents and families are the life blood of new audiences!

Chapter Five

One of the unique features of the Watermill is its setting. At what other theatre, early in the morning, literally at crack of dawn, could you watch the mist rise off the river as the heron slowly walks downstream, fishing as he goes; watch a deer come to the water's edge to drink; catch the flash of blue of a kingfisher darting up river; enjoy the ducks dabbling in the shallows as the swans glide by with their cygnets? Work has often come to a halt or been momentarily disrupted as a result of the wildlife. There was the occasion when a baby squirrel fell out of the theatre's grid, landing on stage during a performance; the discovery in a dressing room that a squirrel or a field mouse had taken a liking to the toe caps on a particularly fine pair of spats and gnawed right through them; the sparring of two cob swans defending their territory in the car park being parted in the end with a hose; a huge flock of Canada geese and their young – literally hundreds of them all swimming round the mill pool; the mole and the mink brought into our office by our cats; the death of many kingfishers, who foolishly used to sit on a wall overlooking the river to fish – but within paw-splatting reach of one of our cats – or failed to understand windows; there was also the occasion when – not exactly wildlife – one of our neighbour's cows – found its way into our car park and sat heavily on our small, newly planted lilac tree! The height and maturity of its replacement is a reminder of just how many years ago that is.

But of course the Watermill wouldn't be the same without its ducks. We had a brief foray with eight beautiful Khaki Campbells before the fox came a-visiting, but we had been at the Watermill for over ten years before we decided to introduce Muscovy ducks to the gardens. We were initially given eight tiny balls of fluff that seemed awfully young to be away from their parents, but they survived and prospered and were soon joined by four other orphaned tufted ducks. Since then ducks and ducklings have become part of the fixtures and fittings. Audience members arrive with bread for them and also are persuaded into sharing their ice creams at the interval, which the big male Muscovies particularly enjoy. We even went as far as to introduce an 'adopt a duck' fund-raising scheme. For just £10 you received a biography of your duck and a picture, which you could present at the theatre in exchange for an ice cream or a small bag of corn to give to your duck in the interval! It was only when the fox visited too often and the letters of condolence got out of hand that we gave the scheme up. However, it raised over £300 for the theatre. The Watermill just wouldn't be the same without them!

Another incident with the same neighbour's bulls could have had much more serious consequences. In 1985 we were approached by an independent television producer to see if we would be interested in co-producing a play using a story based around *The Archers* – the famous BBC Radio 4 serial. This collaboration turned out to be an unforgettable experience and successful beyond our wildest dreams. The then producer of *The Archers*, William Smethurst, co-ordinated the story and the cast were chosen with some care, as not all the radio cast could be seen as their characters on stage and indeed some had never even acted on a stage. Rather than just do a play in the theatre, we suggested that the Watermill's location could provide the ideal setting for a promenade production and our neighbours at Bagnor Manor, Shona and Donald Campbell, happily joined in by letting us use their Dutch barn and a field for the show. It was a rocky ride to the first performance, in fact the whole thing was nearly called off with three weeks to go, as it all seemed such a disaster.

However, thank heavens, we kept our nerve and it turned into a huge hit with people coming from all over the country to see it. Our Box Office could barely cope with the number of calls and even BT were so concerned at the log jam at the exchange that they were calling us regularly to find out what was going on. The popularity of *The Archers* was amazing. This was the first of many outside promenade shows. We started in the theatre, which was transformed into the Ambridge Village Hall, where the Christmas Variety Show was being rehearsed. Jill Archer decided on a whim that there had to be a fire drill and when she rang the bell we ushered all the audience out onto the front lawn. Once there, Clarie appeared on the opposite side of the river, saying there had been a terrible accident up at the farm and Joe Grundy had been injured by a fall of hay. Everyone was needed to help. So saying, she raced off up the riverbank to the manor, while we organised the audience to walk through the car park and up the back lane to the farm. Those, who were elderly or infirm, were taken on a tractor and low loader set out with hay bales for seating, driven by our Theatre Carpenter, Pete Brown, and Phil Archer. Eddie Grundy was already at the scene of the accident when the audience arrived. Somehow, Clare, who was still our Production Manager, had persuaded the St John's Ambulance to turn up with an ambulance every night, arriving at speed up the lane with the siren blaring, having waited for their entrance cue at the Blackbird pub! Joe Grundy was whisked away, while Shula and Nigel arrived on a bicycle to sell ice creams and then guided everyone back down the lane to take part in the Ambridge Fair, which was happening in the field adjacent to the car park. There was a beer tent, St Bart's school band provided the music, there was a welly-wanging competition and dancing round the maypole and the WI provided a produce stall. Of course the beer tent became the Watermill bar.

One evening we had just got the audience safely into the field when the huge Friesian bull escaped from the next door field! Fortunately he was relatively docile and was secured without mishap to the 200 audience members! After the jamboree in the field everyone returned to the theatre for the Christmas entertainment – an unexplained jump in time but not one that anyone seemed very bothered about. Looking back on it all it was a triumph of stage management by Clare and her team, all linked by radio, and dressed in wellies with wheelbarrows and shotguns to look the part! I can see them now. It was truly magic and a unique, unforgettable use of the location. The production had a brief further life in a slightly altered form in Battersea Park of all places, but it never quite matched up to the real life countryside setting.

Chapter Six

The Archers was the first of many productions to embrace an outside scenario. There is something very English about challenging our inclement weather pattern. Each year, when discussing the possibility of venturing outside, we say we won't do it again, but somehow we get tempted. As audiences' tastes change, as theatre changes and rises to the challenges of audiences, who have ever more choices available to them, so we have mounted productions that have – in our terms anyway – something epic about them. They have a different experience to offer, they broaden people's perceptions and take them away from the usual tunnel vision theatre to make them look laterally and consider things from a different standpoint.

I think this was particularly true of Edward Hall's *Henry V*, which told Shakespeare's story through the eyes of a group of squaddies, who arrived at the theatre in camouflage gear from down the river. The journey to Southampton brought the audience out onto the lawn, the Governor of Harfleur addressed Henry from the roof of the theatre, Princess Kate's English lesson took place in a bath over the river and the Dauphin arrived at the French court astride a horse on the back lawn – a retired police horse loaned to us by the International League for the Protection of Horses. But the real *coup de théâtre* was to take the audience back inside for the battle of Agincourt, where theatrical effects could make up for the lack of soldiers!

Having a horse as one of the company was a first for all of us. Once again our neighbours kindly lent us an adjacent field and stable for Marley, our police horse. An elderly gentleman, he just required a gentle hack every now and again. Unfortunately, what we didn't know was that he had an old back injury, which manifested itself one day when he collapsed beneath my daughter, who was exercising him. A traumatic couple of hours ensued outside the Blackbird pub with a group of people taking it in turns to support and keep him standing until the vet eventually allowed him to be walked very slowly back to his stable. His acting days were obviously numbered, but the League was fantastic and came to collect him and replaced him with an understudy, Eve! She had once been the leader of the Metropolitan Police Display Team at the Royal Tournament and the only caveat to our being able to have her was that she could not be trotted near to brick walls... Her star turn had been to leap through 'a ring of fire' hoops painted to look like a brick wall! The Dauphin's arrival on Eve every evening was a resounding success. We loved having Eve to look after and it was a very sad day when she had to leave us at the end of the run.

All the productions that have been partly staged outside have been special for their very audacity. *A Killing Time* was a murder mystery that required the audience to vote for the identity of the murderer. The murder actually took place in the garden at a garden fête, where all the stall holders – and we had lots – thanks to volunteers from the Friends of the Watermill, who were dressed in white hoods and robes like the Ku Klux Klan. The body was spotted as it floated away down the river as the climax to Act I. Usually the stage management placed a net downstream to catch the body. One night, however, they completely overlooked this and the body was left to float on. It nearly caused someone to have a major heart attack next morning when it was discovered caught in the sluices at the trout farm at the far end of the village. A great story for the Press though, and it actually featured as a question on BBC Radio 4's News Quiz! Fame indeed.

Cold Comfort Farm saw the Friends again taking part, this time as 'the shivering brethren' and guests at a ball, where they had to make their entrance down a flight of stairs we had constructed over the herbaceous border from the bar onto the main lawn. The heroine disappearing to London on the back of a very old tractor was also a sight to be seen, as was the sukebind, a massive climbing plant, which wondrously grew very gradually all over the auditorium on cue! Our stage manager at the time spent weeks coating thick rope in sticky latex and green paint – the magic of theatre! It amazed the audience every time.

The Winter's Tale was another production that worked well with the court scenes taking place inside the theatre and all of Bohemia with Perdita and Florizel out in the garden. So that audiences would know that they would be going outside, we put a tag line to the title *The Winter's Tale – and the Sheepshearing in the Garden by the River* by William Shakespeare! This new title for a Shakespeare play made *Private Eye*! There were a few disgruntled patrons, who came just to see the sheep shearing, expecting the real thing every night, rather than an act from Shakespeare's play celebrating the Festival of Sheep Shearing! We did, however, have a couple of rare breed sheep loaned to us for the occasion

41

to add authenticity – they had a lot of visitors over the five-week run and the lawn took some time to recover.

More recently we ventured outside with *A Clandestine Marriage*, *Love in a Maze*, *The Triumph of Love* and *Thieves' Carnival*. They all had their inside alternatives in case of rain, but we only had to resort to that once or twice for each production. This is not the case of course with another open air project. Since 2000 we have collaborated with the people of Boxford, and the local writer Geraldine McCaughrean, to re-stage the pre-Great War Boxford Masques high on Hoar Hill overlooking the Lambourn valley. The Masques were written originally by a former actress, Charlotte Peake, and rediscovered by Boxford resident John Vigor. Charlotte was married to local historian Harold Peake in the Edwardian era. Charlotte's original Masques were extraordinary, pagan yet moral, old fashioned and yet speaking of so many issues affecting us today. These two (so far) large-scale musical community shows, reinvented by Geraldine and led by Ade Morris, have involved upwards of sixty people a time and have proved a huge success and summer celebration of that fantastic Watermill tradition of taking the drama outside. The Masques are now an established Charity under the chairmanship of Euan Smith with his resolute Boxford team. Oh and so far it hasn't rained more than a few drops – that's the magic of Boxford!

Chapter Seven

The Friends of the Watermill are a vital part of the Watermill family. They were formed in the early '80s and we now have over 800 members. They raise funds for the theatre by organising events – Burns Night Celebrations, Supper Talks, Meet the Cast party nights and Theatre visits have all become regular features of the annual calendar, as indeed has the now infamous Summer Fair, held on the first Sunday in June each year. A small, hard-working committee inevitably does most of the organising and in recent years their fund-raising target has grown and grown. It now stands at an impressive £35,000 a year! This is an incredibly important contribution to the theatre's coffers, but, more than that, it represents a committed group of people, who value the theatre and support its work as regular audience members and advocates.

All Friends organisations need a President and for many years, until his death in 1995, we were fortunate in having Sir Michael Hordern in that role. However, he wasn't always that friendly towards the theatre... He came to live in Bagnor in the 1950s and in fact nearly bought the mill for £3,000, but was warned off it by an over-zealous surveyor friend, who told him that at the very least the roof would need replacing, as it was rotten. He instead bought a cottage in the village where he came to fish and to escape theatre! Imagine his despair when the Gollins bought the mill and turned it into just what he was trying to forget...

When we moved in he came to wish us well, but said in his inimitable way that he didn't approve of what we were doing and he wouldn't be coming to any of the shows. A couple of years later we put on a production of *The Killing of Sister George* and the wonderful Peggy Mount came down to play the lead. She and Michael were old friends, so he was tempted to come and support her, encouraged by his wife Eve. It was Peggy's practice to sit and enjoy a bottle of wine with friends after the show at a table outside the front of the theatre and on this particular night she and Michael had been talking well into the night. As James went to turn out the lights of the theatre at about one in the morning, he came across Michael walking up the lawn dripping wet, but being English Gentlemen neither of them brought attention to it, but wished each other 'goodnight'. It was the next day that Michael admitted to having swayed down to the river to relieve himself after saying good night to Peggy and he had fallen in head first! From that moment on he became a firm friend and came to see every production – and indeed became President. The roof, incidentally, was re-tiled in 1986 and the timbers were in pristine condition, not a sign of rot!

Chapter Eight

Two major productions in the early 1980s cannot go by un-noted. Our son, Sam was born in February 1983 and our daughter Charley two years later in January 1985.

I have no doubt that, having our own family growing up at the theatre and very much part of the life of the companies we brought together for each show, has contributed to the spirit of the place. I always remember overhearing an actor who'd worked for us several times, describing the place to a newcomer and saying: 'Of course Jill and James have a huge family'. When this was queried he continued, 'We're all part of the family, everyone who's ever worked here'. Indeed, I think Sam and Charley were very fortunate in having this extended family as they grew up. We have many happy memories of performances being created on the lawn when they were tiny, adventures in the back waters of the river on the boat – like *The African Queen* – or crayfish trapping, rounders picnics up at Snelsmore Common, celebrating birthdays and of course there was the memorable day when we decided that the watercress and weed in the river had got out of control and we organised a river clearing spaghetti party with Paul Clayton, Val and Kazia Pelka, Jenny Galloway, Clare and Nicola Russell – our PR rep – and Teddy Hutton and countless others. We were frozen to the marrow with lacerated hands from the paper like cuts of thin razor-sharp reeds, but all able to appreciate a free-flowing and triumphant river by dusk!

One tradition that we have kept going production by production has been the 'dress rehearsal supper'. Over the years James and I have cooked hundreds of meals for the actors and stage management after a dress rehearsal at the end of a long day of technical rehearsals. Some of those recipes and memories may one day form the basis of another book, as they tell their own story of changing fashions from the days of lamb stew casseroles to exclusively vegetarian meals – and now dairy-free creations of course to accommodate my dietary fads!

Those suppers have always been kept completely separate from the Watermill's restaurant, a vital part of the financial equation that keeps the theatre running. Many a time over the years, as we have staggered from crisis to crisis with the catering, I have wished that we could have made financial sense of making it a franchise – but it was not to be. However, we have had moments of calm amongst the storms! At the start, Andrea Leeman and Tessa Baker began the task of establishing a new order. It hasn't been easy. We have had many catering managers – one Chef Manager, who shall remain nameless, was particularly alarming, wielding kitchen knives and getting quite excited when asked to leave after a particularly hairy incident! There was the occasion when the Chef and the Catering Manager walked out on the same day, leaving us really up the creek! It was seven weeks before we found replacements and during that time it was like living in Fawlty Towers – if only the audience had known that there was another performance happening in the kitchen when they arrived to eat in the restaurant before or after the show!

I took on the cooking with sous chefs, talented actresses, Kazia Pelka and Jenny Galloway, whilst Euan

Smith became our Restaurant Manager, calmly looking after the customers...while hysteria reigned nightly in the kitchen. It was an amazing time – we always seemed to be very busy, cooking for vast numbers at every sitting. I also discovered that adding to my tiredness was the fact that I had caught chicken pox from the children!

I have never had to cook again, but I have had to be Catering Manager as well as Artistic Director – and boy were those long days, crying over trying to get the banking correct at the end of business at one in the morning. There were also the odd matinees when no waiting staff turned up and Sheena Marsh, our then Admin Secretary, and Kate Bishop, our Box Office Manager, would save the day when the coach parties arrived for lunch! Catering Managers Ray Joliffe, Henk de Vries and Lizzie King all made their memorable and much appreciated marks in one way of the other, but credit for the present smooth running of the bar and restaurant must go to Clare Lindsay – who having left us in 1986 as Production Manager, returned to us in 2001, having a sabbatical from theatre, to re-organise and re-focus the operation. With Chef, Grahame Simmonds, they were a formidable team until Clare understandably decided it was time to return to theatre administration and make way for a new Catering Manager, Peter Driscoll. Unfortunately, people have long memories as far as food is concerned. I understand this, but for the last few years Grahame has produced some stunning food and, whenever we get the opportunity, we urge lapsed customers to give us another try and, when they do, they are rarely disappointed and pass the good word on. Reputations are all too easily lost and our chef deserves for that to be turned around, particularly as we now have a new Catering Manager leading the team, the fantastic Clement Otieno.

Chapter Nine

When I first came to the Watermill, having spent the majority of my professional life in touring theatre, I was determined that the Watermill would travel overseas and tour in this country too. So much time and effort goes into creating shows that it always seemed to me a terrible waste to let things disappear after only a few weeks of life. As I write this the touring side of our work has developed in a way that I never imagined could be possible. Indeed last year we were awarded a three-year National Touring Contract by Arts Council England to take at least one production a year to middle and large scale theatres all over the country. Quite an accolade for a small under-funded theatre in the country – we may be small, but we have big aspirations!

Our very first overseas tour was in the 1980s with *The Merchant of Venice*, which went to India, Pakistan, Sri Lanka, Nepal and Iraq under the auspices of the British Council. This was a tricky start to our new relationship with the British Council. The production took time to get together and we had actually foolishly agreed to open in Bombay, just doing a dress rehearsal at the British Council's theatre space in London. I went out for the opening in Bombay and once it was underway all went well. Clare Lindsay, our then Production Manager, remembers the experience well! A company including Meg Davies, Kathryn Hunter, Celia Imrie and Bernard Kay played sixteen venues in ten weeks to packed houses with overwhelming hospitality.

With everything travelling excess baggage and called a 'suitcase' tour, three Elizabethan-style fibreglass trunks contained set, props, lighting and costumes! And, as the tour progressed, more and more souvenirs added to the excess! Considering the many challenges and the difficult start, all went remarkably smoothl,y with the only major hiccup being getting into Iraq. Having been told that the visas would be picked up on arrival in Baghdad, the company were not allowed to join their flight, as they had no Iraqi visas. After a lot of string-pulling by the British Council, twenty-four hours later the company were on their way and the Baghdad performances went ahead on schedule.

Since 1983 we have visited over twenty-four countries worldwide, from Brazil to Japan and from Mexico to Bangladesh! In 1998 we took our all-male version of *Henry V* to Germany to the Neuss Shakespeare Festival and the re-creation of a Globe Theatre. The original concept behind the production, which moved from the theatre into the gardens of the Watermill and back again, was that it should be able to be played anywhere and we would move the audience from location to location, wherever we were. The story propelled forward with such velocity from the start, that taking the audience outside to go to France was the most natural thing in the world. The excitement and anticipation in the audience – even a foreign audience – was electrifying and the pure enjoyment was paramount, even when it rained. The whole show was portable and travelled as excess baggage. It packed into three large flight cases, two punch bags and an ammunition box, which contained the guns and swords. As I write, this tour was less than ten years ago – what huge and impossible problems this would cause today!

The Globe was the perfect setting. Seating 400 to 500 people on three levels, the theatre itself was sited within the grounds of a racecourse in a wooded area just outside Düsseldorf. The outside shingled area, where they put tables and chairs for interval drinks, proved the perfect outside setting – a little re-positioning of the tables to form a parallel traverse walkway, embracing an area where the audience could gather, and a raised area for Katherine's bath, was all that was needed.

Rainer Wiertz, the Festival Director and his assistant, Andreas Giessen, were initially very sceptical about the production working outside. They thought that once the theatre doors were opened the audience would head straight for the bar – they became even more worried as we rehearsed in the pouring rain! However, an audience of just over 400 arrived and, from the moment the play started, the company had them eating out of the palms of their hands. An intelligent audience, who knew their Shakespeare, reacted with delight and enthusiasm to both the verbal and the visual moments. The evening rain cleared, so that, when the moment came to go outside, it was bright and rain free. No-one went to the bar – the whole audience did as they were instructed and followed the actors outside touring the unusual locations. The audience loved it and returned with even more anticipation for what might happen in the second half. The response at the end was phenomenal, as 400 Germans erupted into the English football chant as they stood and applauded the company at the curtain call.

The get-out was completed swiftly and the evening ended with a communal supper outside, where only an hour before Henry V had been rallying his troops. Our thoughts turned with some trepidation to the next day and our long journey to Brandenburg in the former East Germany.

Rather like the England football team we travelled by coach and arrived after nine hours in a small town called Kyritz. What a different world it was. The affluence of the West disappeared swiftly and cobbled streets appeared. There were a lot of car companies moving in, the inevitable McDonalds and other ubiquitous multinational chains on the outskirts of towns. But in the villages and small towns the houses were dilapidated, although tidily kept, and we passed many grim-looking, barrack-style housing blocks all fenced off. The hotel in Kyritz, however, was beautiful and we settled there in comfortable rooms before being taken to the tiny village of Drewen, where we were to perform one show as part of their arts festival. Started six years previously, it was officially a music and visual arts festival and we were to be their first ever dramatic offering. Our stage was a simple farmyard and very ad hoc – I imagine it looked rather like the Watermill might have done thirty years previously.

All the farm buildings around had been utilised for exhibition spaces for an extreme and amazing range of modern art. A large barn had been converted into a studio for piano recitals – with shades of the early years at the Watermill. The whole experience was very esoteric and bizarre, and strangely familiar! It poured with rain all afternoon and we never thought an audience would arrive, but, come 7.30, people began to wander in – whole families coming for a night out. There was one couple, who seemed completely out of place. Dressed in long cream belted raincoats they entwined themselves round each other and gazed into each other's eyes, talking intently. Then as suddenly as they had arrived, they got up and left – before the performance even started! There must have been about 100 people in that East German square – and remarkably they seemed to enjoy the spectacle of old European history, played out in Shakespearean English, by British blokes dressed as women, in the open farmyard air of a rapidly changing world – particularly the entrance of the Dauphin on a locally borrowed horse! And even the weather again miraculously cleared, so that we had a rain free, idyllic evening, which ended in a massive barbecue and party. The next day we rather reluctantly returned in our magic coach to the West – it was almost as though it had all been a dream!

The most extensive tour was undertaken in 1998, when, under the wing of the British Council, we toured with *Henry V* and *The Comedy of Errors* to Mexico, Italy, Germany, Bangladesh, Sri Lanka, Indonesia, The Philippines and Malaysia. What an outstanding success that was. For those of us managing the tour from England, it was also quite alarming, as once the company headed to the Far East, they travelled through several war zones and in Bangladesh the country was experiencing the worst flooding the nation had ever experienced. In Jakarta it was riots, with the company confined to the hotel and only able to get to the theatre for the performance at the very last minute. The relentless schedule also resulted in a great deal of sickness and hurriedly improvised understudying from within the company as the heavy schedule took its toll, but nevertheless they all returned triumphant and eager for more!

This was in the early days of Propeller, when we still packed everything into half a dozen portable skips and took everything with us on flights as excess baggage. Amazingly we played in locations as diverse as that farm yard in East Germany to a 2000-seat conventional proscenium arch theatre in the Philippines. The large parts of the action, which took place outside the theatre, were happily accepted everywhere, as audiences willingly followed the actors into adjacent car parks or, when in Rome, into the street outside, which the theatre management had got cordoned off for the occasion! Whenever the company added in a few words of the language of the country they found themselves in, audiences were at the actors' feet – such was the charm of the Shakespeare boys! Maybe we have not managed to travel to quite such exotic places since those halcyon days, but return trips to the magical Globe Theatre in Neuss and more visits to Italy, to Rome, Verona and Bologna, as well as Gdansk and Istanbul, Cyprus and Barbados have more than been enjoyed.

Perhaps one of the most exciting moments, and most recent (although it is almost impossible to single just one out), was opening *A Midsummer Night's Dream* in New York at the Harvey Theatre. We were invited to perform there by the Brooklyn Academy of Music, a great honour in itself. But reading the subsequent rave reviews in the *New York Times* and *Wall Street Journal* were moments to be savoured for many a year by a British theatre company.

None of this would have happened if Edward Hall had not accepted an invitation to direct *Othello* back in 1995! I had been looking for new young directors and James had been working with Ed on an overseas tour with the RSC and said to me, 'You must meet him, he's good, you'll like him'. Like him I did, we struck up an immediate rapport and our relationship of mutual respect has grown from strength to strength, resulting eventually in the creation of Propeller, an all-male group of actors in the tradition of Shakespeare's original acting company.

Propeller's aim is simple: to perform Shakespeare with a contemporary aesthetic whilst maintaining the necessary emphasis on the spoken word. Developing the relationship between the performer and the audience in and around the play is of paramount importance, creating some of the atmosphere that must have been a large part of the experience of watching plays in the outdoor theatre in Shakespeare's time. To that end there is a particular emphasis on live music, played and sung by the actors. *Henry V* was the first production and developed from the initial idea that the story would be told by a group of squadies – hence the all-male company and the creation of a unique ensemble in Propeller.

The concept has worked incredibly well, with the nucleus of the company remaining constant throughout and the strength of the ensemble being the extraordinary bond that has been created with everyone involved. There is a total commitment to the work and a strong loyalty to Ed, which binds everyone together. I always think of Propeller and Ed as my 'boys' – very much part of our extended family.

Having spent five of my formative early years with the Royal Shakespeare Company, Shakespeare has always been very important to me. I was lucky enough to have worked as a stage manager with Trevor Nunn, John Barton and Terry Hands and heard the text analysed and broken down in precise detail. It is now equally thrilling to hear Ed talk about the text and together with the boys make it so clear for modern audiences – so much so that the public invariably believe that the text has been re-written.

The Watermill has contributed to the style of the productions with Michael Pavelka's designs and Ben Ormerod's lighting refining and distilling the essence of the work within a small space, and yet still making it possible for the productions to expand into larger theatres. This is all to do with the ensemble's power in storytelling. Get the relationships right on stage and the focus on the actors and expanding is no problem. Propeller's style has proved very popular with young and old alike in audiences all over the world.

I am immensely proud that all but one of these productions has toured and travelled world-wide, with two, *Rose Rage* and *A Midsummer Night's Dream*, receiving highly acclaimed London runs. It's an achievement not only for Ed, Michael, Ben and the boys, but for all the admin and technical staff at the Watermill, who are all part of the ensemble in the background that continues to develop the work. Later in 2005 we are heading off to the Dublin, Canterbury, Madrid and Girona Festivals as well as America, for a return visit to BAM and first visits to California and Washington. In the New Year we head East again to China and beyond – the fantastic journey continues!

Touring in England is something we have developed gradually – visiting other theatres for maybe one or two weeks, not planned very far in advance has now been developed thanks to the National Touring Contract to the extent that we plan the touring alongside our main programme of work. Touring is important for a number of reasons – extending the life of a production is good for all those, who get extra employment out of it; it makes sense in terms of value for money; it helps to build the ambassadorial skills of everyone involved; exposes the show and the company to a variety of audiences all over the country; it addresses problems of rural isolation and access through lack of public transport in rural areas; it generates income and broadens sponsorship opportunities; and it raises the profile of the theatre and the work in general. Lots of boxes ticked!

But most particularly, there is something very exhilarating about being 'on the road' with a production. Moving into a new theatre every week and re-creating the show for a new audience and packing it away on a Saturday night and setting off for the next date. The rural touring to smaller theatres, village and community halls, which we have also developed over the last four or five years, has likewise been immensely rewarding. We discovered through audience research that twenty-five per cent of those audiences would not otherwise attend theatre at all! It has also become our regular outlet for new writing. On these small-scale tours we have found very receptive audiences, who enjoy knowing that what they get in their village hall has not been seen anywhere else – village communities around Newbury really are at the cutting edge of new writing and this level of touring has become a seedbed for both the building of new theatre audiences and the creation of new plays.

Side by side with the development of rural touring is all the outreach work that is such an important part of our annual programme of work – incorporating, of course, the Watermill Youth Theatre. The expansion into primary school touring, community projects, corporate workshops, summer school workshops, primary school projects and business training workshops and seminars has all been instigated in partnership with our current Outreach Director, Ade Morris. Projects with the West Berkshire Federation of Village Schools and the Downs Federation have involved over a hundred young children in each production, which have been written from ideas and thoughts explored by the children in pre-production workshops with Ade as writer and a visual artist – very frequently Julieann Worrall Hood.

For the week that the children are performing at the theatre, portacabins in the car park provide dressing room accommodation and the whole event is like a military operation. Each village school within the federation gets its chance to shine, but also, because of the involvement of the visual artist, both theatre and schools have been left with physical mementos. The Green Man in the corner of the garden is a living willow, which hopefully will be there for years to come, as will the barbed wire baby and the stained glass window.

A workaholic like the rest of us, Ade has also been responsible for the majority of the new writing that has taken place for young people at the Watermill, for the Young Company and for small-scale touring over the last few years, supplemented by plays from Ben Myers and now Will Wollen for the Youth Theatre. Ade's personal development as a writer is something we have nurtured and his writing has matured and flowered as a result of his being able to see his work performed regularly – an opportunity so few writers get. *I Dreamt I Dwelt in Marble Halls* is based on a lovely Bryan Gallagher short story, which I heard broadcast on the late John Peel's

'Home Truths' one Saturday morning in 2001, and helped establish both Ade as a new writer and the Watermill as a leading sponsor of such new writing. It transferred with great success to the Tricycle Theatre in London. Our small-scale tours now travel the length and breadth of England, Wales and Ireland, as well as delighting our crucial West Berkshire rural-based audiences twice a year – another crucial spoke in the Watermill wheel.

Having the opportunity to support new and emerging talent is immensely satisfying. As a producing theatre, we have the facility to nurture and provide a safe haven for the new generation of creative artists, technicians and administrators. This is born from a belief that artistic creativity needs to be fed regularly by new ideas and the exploration of new practices – it is a continuous evolutionary process. It involves taking calculated risks with talented individuals, who I believe will respond to nurturing in a secure and professionally supported environment.

Apart from touring, one of James' and my shared passions is for musical theatre. This was not something that had been included in the Watermill year very often when we arrived, so it was very important to us that it featured strongly in our programming.

One of my favourites was *Once Upon a Mattress* by Mary Rogers, in which a very young Sally Dexter and Douglas Hodge starred – this was a wonderfully mad romp directed by Wendy Toye. Then there was the first time that we staged Stephen Sondheim's *Sweeney Todd*. A phenomenal success, but what a nightmare journey to the first performance! Firstly, our Sweeney was taken ill at the start of rehearsals and had to be replaced, fortunately for us, by the wonderful Neil McCaul. Then our Mrs Lovett suffered a nervous breakdown and couldn't be persuaded to return for the final week of rehearsals. This meant that we had to delay the opening in order to give Lesley Duff, her replacement, a few days' rehearsal! This, however, resulted in the director having to withdraw, as he was contracted to start another show before our new opening! So, two new leads, a delayed opening night and now a new director!

Some may have given up at this point, but we had to present something in the theatre and, as the show was coming together so well, we decided not to be daunted and, with the blessing of the rest of the cast, to find a new director. And find one we did – Timothy Prager agreed to take up the challenge and we set sail for an opening delayed by ten days. I'll never forget the dress rehearsal night, the day before we were due to open to a sold out Saturday matinee. The Judge had just had his throat cut and had slid sedately from the barber's chair to the cellar beneath. Then there was a moment of complete and utter stillness when you just know that something dreadful has happened! I flew backstage to discover the Judge, with his leg doubled up beneath him, in complete agony. The ambulance arrived within five minutes and he was rushed to the local hospital. Covered with blood from just having had his throat cut, you can understand why the hospital reacted to a horrific head wound rather than a leg injury!

Fortunately, all was sorted swiftly – Steve O'Hara had not broken his leg, but had badly strained all the ligaments in his foot and lower leg, so that he was unable to walk. The hospital reacted brilliantly to the situation and assured us that they could fix a walking cast on Steve's leg, so that he could put some weight on it and be able to walk – all be it with the aid of crutches. So the first performance was able to go ahead with a few crucial adjustments as to who went down the barber's chair chute!

When I scheduled *Sweeney Todd* again, many people asked me whether I thought it was wise, considering what had happened previously! However, it was a piece that I thought would lend itself so well to the actor/musician style of production and also it was one of John Doyle's favourites. And how glad I am that we did decide to do it again. A wonderful cast played here at the Watermill and then toured for six weeks before transferring to the Trafalgar Studios in London (the old Whitehall Theatre) for a limited run and from there to the New Ambassadors. The production with a cast of American actors led by Patti LuPone and Michael Cerveris opened on Broadway in November 2005. A wonderful coincidence for the Watermill was that *The Winter's Tale* opened at the Harvey Theatre on Wednesday November 2nd and was followed on the 3rd by *Sweeney Todd* on Broadway. Quite an achievement for a small English producing theatre to have instigated two New York openings in two days!

Every year we have staged a piece of music theatre and they all have their particular memories. In 1988, *Songbook* by Julian More and Monty Norman, which had premiered in Cambridge when I was there, proved the perfect piece around which to build the celebrations for the theatre's 21st birthday. A huge marquee on the lawn and dinner for two hundred with HRH Prince Edward was a huge success. This was followed by a second royal gala four years later when we celebrated twenty-five years, again with Prince Edward, with a performance of

The Card with Peter Duncan (now Chief Scout) playing the lead – a production not without its dramas. It was a co-production with Cameron Mackintosh – I had been on the technical course with Cameron at the Central School many years before – and all was going well until we had had to change directors a week into rehearsals, because Paul Kerryson damaged his back and couldn't stand upright. We were incredibly fortunate on that occasion to have Jeremy Sams as his replacement. The music and original lyrics for the show had been written by Tony Hatch and Jackie Trent and I remember on the occasion of our 25th birthday celebrations we had an impromptu cabaret after dinner in the marquee – I have vivid memories of all two hundred guests singing Tony and Jackie's most well known song 'Neighbours' in raucous unison at one in the morning – including HRH!

Some of the lyrics for *The Card* had been re-written by Anthony Drewe, who I had first met when introduced to him and his writing partner George Stiles by Cameron. He asked whether we would consider staging Stiles and Drewe's new musical *Just So*. This had just won a prize in the Vivien Ellis Awards and Cameron wanted to try it out with a full-scale production. We fell in love with the piece instantly and felt it would be a huge success, even though completely unknown. It needed work before it could be staged and also needed a production budget that was beyond our means, so a co-production with the Mackintosh organisation was essential in order to get it on. Julia McKenzie directed and the show was designed by Mark Thompson. We built a second rehearsal space on the lawn, so that we could have double rehearsals going all the time. It was a nightmare scaffolding construction which leaked constantly whenever it rained, which it seemed to do a great deal of the time. That show really did prove the point that musicals are not just written, but re-written and re-written. It transferred to the Tricycle in London, where it received substantial re-writes, and after that it was seen in many guises in various productions in the States before most recently having another full scale and substantially re-written outing at Chichester Festival Theatre. But for all the re-writing, it was very familiar and seeing it fifteen years later, was a very nostalgic experience. A great show – witty lyrics and some wonderfully haunting melodies.

We have worked several times with George and Ants over the years – we commissioned them to write *The Ugly Duckling* for us for a Christmas show. This has since been re-named *Honk!* and has had over a thousand successful productions worldwide, including the National Theatre. Together they wrote for us a terrific revue entitled *Warts and All*, and individually George composed and arranged the music for *Moll Flanders*, while Ants has displayed his talents also as an actor in *Rogues to Riches* and as a director for *Snoopy*.

Recently our musical work has become much more 'music theatre' than 'musical theatre' as we have concentrated on working with John Doyle and an evolving team of actor/musicians. I had worked with John once previously, when he directed *Tom Jones* here, and I was aware of the work he had been doing at Liverpool and York with actor/musicians. *Cabaret* had for a long time been a favourite of mine and I was convinced that it could work well in the Watermill space with actor/musicians. I wanted to turn the whole theatre into the Kit Kat Club and tell the story from that premise – and that's just what we did, with seats removed and cabaret tables dotted around the acting area. Well, it worked superbly, winning the 1998 Barclays TMA Theatre Award for Best Musical. Richly deserved by a superb cast.

This was the start of a long and productive relationship with John. Each year we have presented a new piece – *Irma La Douce, Carmen, The Gondoliers, Ten Cents a Dance, Fiddler on the Roof, A Star Danced, Sweeney Todd, Pinafore Swing* and this year *Mack and Mabel* – the last seven in partnership with brilliant musical director Sarah Travis. Interspersed with the main season work, we have also presented some delightful Christmas shows, all original scripts by John and with music by Sarah Travis or Cathy Jayes – apart from *Sinbad*, which was written by Christopher Lillicrap – *Cinderella and the Enchanted Slipper, Beauty and the Beast, Sinbad* and *The Wizard of Oz* – all with actor/musicians – a style of work that originally grew out of economic necessity, but certainly since *Cabaret* days has become a specific choice. Actors sing, dance, act and play instruments – their instruments become part of the character, it becomes the most natural thing in the world for Mrs Lovett in *Sweeney Todd* to be playing a trumpet or for Joanna to accompany herself on the cello! The success of *Sweeney Todd* in London has given this very Watermillesque genre the wider showcase it deserves and will hopefully open the doors for many future productions in London and elsewhere.

Like the work with Ed and Propeller, working with John and Sarah has been really special – so much so that I decided I would commission John and Sarah to write a completely new piece. So *A Star Danced* was born, inspired by the story of *Much Ado About Nothing* – a connection with a well known piece, which we hoped would give the audience some security. It was really exciting to see a completely new piece grow from scratch and for it to be such a success. Rewarding not only for John and Sarah, but for me to see two really talented people getting the opportunity to put their own creation on stage here. If getting a new piece of writing produced is difficult, it is only surpassed by getting a second opportunity for a new piece. Writers continually have that frustration – new work grows during performance, and I only hope that *A Star Danced* will one day be given another chance to enable it to grow further.

Chapter Ten

The period before, during, and immediately after the building of the by-pass I recall with a certain sense of disbelief – it was a surreal period, when our lives were disrupted by strangers, when the normally peaceful, tranquil countryside surrounding us was torn apart by alien beings from unknown places. Squads of police and security men decided how we lived. Our audience was confused as to whether or not we were open – as the main road to the village was frequently impassable. Even if notices convinced that the road was open, there was a certain alarm as to what would happen if confronted by the remarkable 'tree people'!

Bog Camp was just at the end of the village, desperately trying to protect an area of ancient woodland that was soon to meet with the chain saw. I remember one early morning when police and security men marched into Bagnor to join forces with the mechanical 'cherry pickers' in removing those camped in the trees. The screams were piercing and desperate – signalling despair that they could not hold out any longer against officialdom and brute force.

I admit to openly weeping that morning as trees were felled in front of us. Precious areas of woodland gone in the name of progress. Being there and seeing it happen, seeing well-meaning people hauled out of trees was something I'll never forget. It's not the same when you see it reproduced on television – the impact cannot be recaptured – the physical pain gets glossed over, sanitised by professional reporting, which takes the emotion out of the story. It was probably over a period of four years when we lived through the prelude of protest to the crescendo, as tarmac gradually forced its way through – a period which I'll never forget and which changed the area for ever.

Once the camps had been dismantled, the whole area was surrounded by wire fencing and patrolled by security guards – what a contrast to the quiet leafy country lane that had once led down to the village. Floodlights destroyed the darkness at night for months to come – no wonder our audience attendance figures dropped so dramatically, as everyone avoided the area while it was all under construction.

Thankfully, in the long term, it has had little effect on the theatre, though we who lived here before can hear the traffic intruding on the peace and quiet. We can remember the beauty of Snelsmore Common and the track leading to it, which provided such a brilliant toboggan run in the winter months, and the magical, leafy, tree–lined lane that led down to the village. For the average punter, however, the Watermill has retained its charm. Once you leave the road behind and cross over the bridges into Bagnor, you can still, for a while, forget progress and be enraptured by the timeless peace and tranquility of the Watermill grounds – particularly in the spring and the summer, when the sound of the wind in the trees supercedes every noise created by traffic.

Sitting beside the river on a still summer's afternoon, looking at the mill, you can almost see and hear the people, who have been part of this complex for nearly 200 years. It may have been tidied up and had bits added on, but the fabric of the place, the soul of the bricks themselves is rich with the history of people over two centuries. Even now with the hum of the bypass in the background, nothing can disturb completely the tranquility that pervades this little corner of Berkshire. The constant force of the river brings an almost mystical quality to the peace here, the journey of the water constantly regenerating and invigorating life along its path.

It was while all the bypass dramas were happening that a Theatre Review was carried out in the South of England with the aim of re-aligning funding. With the by-pass difficulties, we were already in fighting mood, so when we learned that it had been proposed that the Watermill should no longer receive core funding, but apply for project funding instead, it was like putting a match to the blue touch paper! It would have meant the theatre eventually closing, if it was no longer supported as a producing theatre. Our Chairman at that time, Angus Crichton-Miller, set up the Waterwings Appeal and we produced mounds of figures, which showed just what value for money the theatre was – how for every £1 of subsidy, the number of performances that were mounted and the number of people who attended exceeded all expectation. We showed that we were producing more work to a higher attendance level than many of our better funded competitors.

Armed with this information, we appealed to our 800-strong Friends of the Watermill and people, who had worked here previously, to write letters of protest about the proposed decision to their MP and to the Chairman of Southern Arts. This letter writing campaign was an outstanding success – the then Chairman of Southern Arts was so inundated with letters he asked us to stop the campaign because a subsequent decision had been made – that the Watermill should indeed retain core funding! Whether the campaign helped or not is neither here nor there – what it did show was an amazing support for the Watermill, which spurred us on even more.

Chapter Eleven

I have tried to convey the essence of the Watermill and the life we have led here. It has been the most extraordinary period, full of so many conflicting emotions. Yet, by necessity, it has had to be a very ordered life. Everything in the end revolves around the 7.30 deadline – the performance. A lot of thought and planning goes into the preparation of the annual programme and yet one must always be ready to act spontaneously. I myself am no actress and withdraw from the limelight – however there was one occasion when it was a case of cancel performances and disappoint hundreds of children or get on there yourself. It was during the run of *Charlotte's Web* and one of the cast, Tessa Pritchard, had been battling with a dreadful cold, which had settled onto her chest. The doctor eventually issued an ultimatum, saying that, if she was to avoid becoming seriously ill, she had to stop performing and rest. Tessa played two parts, so I decided that I would just about be able to cope with one – the goose – and I persuaded our Company Stage Manager, Jan Doyle, to take on the other. I coped because I was able to hide behind a wonderful padded costume with a huge baseball cap for a beak, which hid most of my face, and large flippers for my webs. We had about an hour's notice having come to the decision, so there was barely time to suffer from nerves, let alone to have a rehearsal! But on we went, holding scripts. We both had solo numbers and had to dance, and, although I say it myself, we weren't at all bad! At any rate we kept the show going and most importantly didn't have to turn away all those children. We did five performances altogether – and I was shaking just as much at the final one as I was at the first! How actors willingly go though the trauma every night I will never know – fortunate for me that they do however – otherwise I'd be out of a job!

On another occasion, Ed Hall was visiting and we were discussing the next Shakespeare over lunch, when one of the cast of *Lettice and Lovage* was stricken with heart palpitations and was whisked off to hospital. Although Ed had never seen the show, he offered to go on with the book for the matinee as it was a relatively small role. So with a quick one-hour rehearsal, on he went and a full house of elderly coach parties rose to their feet in appreciation.

John Doyle also helped out on one unforgettable occasion during *The Gondoliers*. Mike Afford had a large part and had struggled against illness for a number of performances before succumbing to the inevitable. So John went on – he didn't play the trumpet like Mike, but the rest of the cast were able to cover for this and John sang and danced his way through the rest of the performance – it was a magic event that I will never forget!

Audiences do respond very positively when they become involved in such dramas – the Dunkirk spirit prevails with everyone and the maxim 'the show must go on' always seems to win through in the end.

I will never forget standing in the foyer at 6.45 pm before a performance of *Blood Brothers*, which had proved an outstanding success, when Louise Gold, who played the lead, came into the foyer to make her way up to the dressing rooms. She was on great form, said 'Hi!' and promptly collapsed writhing at my feet. The emergency services were with us in no time at all – fortunately – as we were to discover that Louise was suffering from an eptopic pregnancy and was seriously ill. We never carry understudies – it is just too expensive – so this did pose a big problem. Louise would not recover to come back to us in time and there were three weeks of sold-out performances ahead of us. It was also August Bank Holiday, so couldn't have been a worse time to try and set up a replacement. However, we thought that, if we could find someone who had played the role relatively recently at another theatre, we would be able to work them into the production quite quickly – the most important requirement was that, whoever came already knew the music. By a miracle we found Gillian Bevan that Friday evening, who knew the part and agreed to help us out for the evening performance on the Saturday. She came down and rehearsed briefly on the Saturday afternoon before going on in the lead – and she was fantastic! Adrenalin was racing through the rest of the cast as well and produced a unique event for the appreciative audience.

However, our concern was to keep to a minimum the number of performances we had to cancel and on the Sunday our telephone search eventually found Elizabeth Power. She had played the part eighteen months previously and agreed to rehearse on the Monday and Tuesday and open on the Wednesday. She performed triumphantly for the rest of the run.

Dilys Hamlett helped us out after the first performance of *Cold Comfort Farm*, when Carole Gillies, who played the grandmother, had to withdraw because of her battle with cancer. Anticipating that this could happen, I had spoken with Dilys in advance and she had been able to get down to see the show at the dress rehearsal. Dilys, who sadly is now no longer with us, was superb.

Richard Clothier was another actor, who stepped 'into the breach', when he took over at the last moment in *The Prisoner of Zenda*, this time when Chris Wells had to fly to South Africa to be with his seriously ill mother. Another great performance achieved in just a few days!

Scary, challenging times indeed. One of the last occasions occurred in recent times when Mike Afford tore his Achilles tendon and had to be replaced in *Cinderella and the Enchanted Slipper*. Again the pressure was to avoid cancelling shows and disappointing young children. By a quirk of fate we made contact with an actor, who lived locally – Andrew Mackintosh. We managed with Mike sitting still at the side of the stage for a couple of performances, while Andrew rehearsed and learnt the role before taking over for the remaining four weeks.

In a similar vein Sean Hennesey was drafted in at the last moment to take over the enormously demanding role of Jimmy Baker in *The Comedian* after the original actor became ill – Sean was the obvious choice, but he was away on holiday in Croatia until the Monday of production week, so we rang round in vain trying to find someone else. When production week started we were still actorless – so Sean bravely went on with the book on Wednesday having had just one day of rehearsal – he attracted rave reviews – particularly for appearing to be 'rehearsing' his comic act so convincingly – prompt script clutched firmly in hand!

I am always amazed that actors are prepared to take such things on at short notice and expose themselves to the judgement of an audience, but on the other hand, the support provided by colleagues and that in-built determination not to disappoint is an exhilarating feeling – I remember it (how could I ever forget it!) from *Charlotte's Web*.

It is depressing that so many excellent actors still spend a greater part of their professional lives resting rather than working. The decline in the number of regional reps has created havoc. Co-productions between theatres reduce the opportunities for new work to be created, affecting everyone, not just actors – but directors, designers, and technicians as well. There are fewer and fewer opportunities for those starting out in the profession. At least the Watermill continues to produce plays year in year out and, by touring, extends the employment opportunities for many. Over the last couple of years, thanks initially to a generous grant from Southern Arts, before it was incorporated into Arts Council England to become South East Arts, we have been able to run a new writing competition, giving six writers on each occasion the opportunity to work with a professional director and actors on a rehearsed reading of their plays. It has been a crucial window of opportunity, not just for the writers, but for young actors and directors too. We continue to work with new writers on script development and hope to bring more and more new work to the stage, indeed we hosted a budding writer from Colombia, Aldemar Restepo, who wrote first in Spanish, then in rapidly emerging English, to produce a new comedy called *The Impossible Club*, which was produced in the rehearsal studio – all of this paid for by a special grant from the British Council.

The last funding crisis came about in 2000, when there came a point when it was impossible to continue to make the figures balance. Everybody at the theatre was working at salaries well below the accepted level and the amount of work being produced was increasing. We were getting just eleven per cent of the income we needed from grants, the rest was being raised through the box office – sixty per cent, catering – four per cent and sponsorship and fund-raising – twenty-five per cent.

The crunch had come – we really had to convince our Regional Arts Board that the theatre needed and deserved better support, otherwise it could not continue. It was a battle that had been waged non-stop since our arrival at the Watermill – we had constantly increased our output without increasing the infrastructure needed to support it, so that the whole organisation was potentially hanging on the edge of a precipice. A financial stock take of the organisation was commissioned to show that the theatre was efficient in all its financial undertakings and to hopefully show where things could be improved in order to free money for increased production budgets and higher salaries.

The stock take in fact showed that there appeared to be nothing else the theatre could do to either generate or save money. William Wilkinson, the retired Royal Shakespeare Company financial controller, concluded that the only hope was for the Watermill to receive proper core funding, sufficient to support a producing theatre. Southern Arts were not satisfied with this response and decided that there should be an artistic and structural survey of the organisation to examine what elements could, if necessary, be cut from the annual programme in order to work within existing grant levels.

It was this survey, led by Kate Devey, that reiterated the fact that the organisation had continued to develop without developing the infrastructure, so that the pressure on the small management team had grown to unacceptable proportions. She concluded that all aspects of the programme were so interwoven, that it would be impossible to cut one element without it having a devastating effect on the whole. She maintained that if the Watermill was going to have a future then it had to have increased core funding to support (a) an increase in salary levels throughout, (b) an increase in management personnel and in particular the employment of a General Manager and (c) an increase in funding to give the theatre more flexibility in setting realistic targets for the box office for each show, rather than the current overall eighty per cent target.

This report proved to be a turning point for the organisation. Everything that we had been working towards over twenty years seemed at last to be recognised as being good and worthwhile. It was also acknowledged that the core funding was extraordinarily low and that everything possible would be done to increase this – to allow us to begin to implement Kate's recommendations. This also coincided with Arts Council England's decision to award the Watermill a National Touring Contract, as already mentioned.

Suddenly we were able to plan more securely in advance, to address the infrastructure of the organisation and to look forward positively to the future. We had always said that, before we left the Watermill we wanted it to have a more stable funding base and for its work to be recognised by the arts bureaucracy. We have now reached that point. It is a strange sensation to have support after years of conflict. It is not easy to relax, because it is almost too good to be true!

However, the theatre still produces an extraordinarily high percentage of earned income – eighty per cent against twenty per cent subsidy – a highly unusual set of figures in the theatre world! So the battle for greater funding and security is still not over by any means. There are other pressures as well, which inevitably come with a higher profile and growing reputation. As we remain focused on the work and maintaining the highest quality in all areas, our opinion is sought and our support asked, we are encouraged, for instance, to build partnerships with other theatres and producers. One result of this is that we are mounting the Christmas show for the New Theatre Royal Portsmouth for the second year running, both former popular Christmas shows staged here at the Watermill. Two other theatres have also approached us to use our expertise in the future and we expect this kind of work to be a growing – an exciting facet of the Watermill to come.

For a small organisation the Watermill has always tried to be at the forefront of new theatrical techniques and developments. Our Production Manager, Lawrence Doyle, has made sure that all the lighting and sound equipment is up to date, state of the art and energy conscious. Lawrence is also a lighting designer and keeps his finger on the pulse of emerging technology. James was determined likewise that the accounts should be computerised as soon as possible – and he slaved hard at that, teaching himself along the way, and eventually saving himself a huge amount of time in keeping the accounts of the organisation under control. For nineteen years until he retired as Touring Director of the Royal Shakespeare Company in 2000, James spent his evenings and weekends looking after all that side of the organisation and keeping it solvent. Through his contacts with the RSC we were also one of the first regional repertory theatres to switch to a computerised box office. When I look back on those years of individual ticket stubs and paper charts for daily performances, I wonder how we ever survived. Now the theatre has its own website and has rapidly growing online ticket sales. We have always avoided the larger box office systems, preferring to be a larger player with a smaller company. James has saved the theatre huge fees over the years with this policy and particularly now that we sell direct through our own website – cutting out the middle man and keeping direct control over the sales. It created lots of headaches whilst it was being set up, but it now means that there are more funds directed straight into the productions rather than into someone else's pocket.

When I look back over the last nearly twenty-five years I can allow myself to be both critical about what has been achieved, but immensely proud at the same time. The journey from those days in the early sixties into the 21st century has been one of considerable achievement both artistically and practically. The battles that have been waged constantly with the arts bureaucracy have been exhausting and ultimately liberating. The Watermill has undoubtedly always suffered by its chocolate box prettiness in a wealthy part of the country. If the work had emanated from an ugly warehouse in an urban complex, I feel with certainty that we would have received adequate grant support many years before. But maybe this is good – we have made possible what many would say was impossible – certainly any businessman looking at the accounts would say that it was a daunting prospect to keep the place afloat. It could only have been achieved by the involvement of people, who were looking for something other than pure financial gain!

Of course we all have to pay the bills in the end, but here at the Watermill we have added riches that cannot easily be quantified. We have produced over 250 productions, thousands of performances, given opportunities to some young artists just starting out on their careers, who are now household names – David Suchet, Bill Nighy, Kathryn Hunter, Sean Bean, Rufus Sewell, Douglas Hodge, Sally Dexter, to name but a few. We have provided a supportive environment in which talented people feel secure and can flourish.

Three particular strands of work for which I know we will be remembered are that of Ed Hall's Propeller, John Doyle's music theatre companies and our work with young people and the community. In the last six years our productions have won several awards and five have transferred for extended runs in London, *The Gondoliers, I Dreamt I Dwelt in Marble Halls, Rose Rage, A Midsummer Night's Dream* and *Sweeney Todd*. Through these shows, all the work has been recognised. It has taken time for that respect to come, but now I feel we are almost part of the establishment! The slightly patronising praise we have had in the past has certainly taken on a different tone. In 1991 we won a Barclays TMA Theatre Award for the Most Welcoming Theatre. I remember in my acceptance speech saying that I hoped next time it would be for the work – and indeed it was to be so! We no longer have to prove that what we do is good, our audiences know it's good and, consequently, the outside world is let in on the secret too. The national press are also now very supportive and will trek out to Berkshire regularly for fodder for both the mind and the body.

What is important to me and I believe for the local community is that all this continues in a similar vein in the future. Whoever takes it on must find their own way of running the place – getting recognition from Arts Council England and South East Arts, so that they continue to fund it, stretching the audiences' imagination, so that they embrace what it has to offer in the future. I believe I have set up a broad enough artistic policy for a newcomer to have the scope to instigate change without frightening the regular audience. It has been my passion for theatre and its ability to communicate that has been my driving force over the years, rooting the artistic programme in the country's strong tradition of text based narrative drama, stimulating the audience's interest in imaginative interpretations of classic texts, epic novels, European work, musical theatre pieces and new writing.

The development of new writing was a little restricted until we found a way, through the rural touring, to really work on it. Previously, presenting new writing in the main auditorium, when high box office attendance was needed, meant that the progress was limited; nevertheless with work adapted by Euan Smith – *Le Grand Meaulnes* (*The Lost Domain*) and *The Prisoner of Zenda* and from Alex Jones – *Deadwood*, we did begin to attract a new writing audience. However, a new found confidence has developed in this area of the main house work because of the success of the new writing on the touring circuit. I recently commissioned a new play by

Alan Plater – *The Last Days of the Empire* for the main auditorium and of course, as already mentioned, there has been John Doyle and Sarah Travis's *A Star Danced*. Next year will also see Ade Morris's new adaptation of *Twenty Thousand Leagues Under the Sea*.

Overall the artistic quality of the work has been key to the theatre's success. I am not interested in the second-rate in any department and, despite the lack of financial resources, the pursuit of excellence has been maintained and achieved throughout. Reviews and audience figures bear testament to this success. Also, and most importantly, has been the support for the new emerging talent. The set up of the Watermill as virtually a small commune effectively provides a residency for artists, giving them rehearsal and playing periods, when they live and work together, creating small individual ensembles, supported by a dedicated team of production, educationalists and administrators, who share the experience of creating theatre on a daily basis. It is this environment that enabled Ed Hall's work to flourish and led to the development of the company into a unique ensemble respected worldwide. It is this whole concept of fostering and nurturing young talent that Kate Devey applauded in her review as a major strength of the theatre, not easily found elsewhere. She stated that this contribution to the development of the individual artist, and consequently to the development of British theatre, should justify wide recognition and support and should be cherished.

It is fascinating to look back on the early years and see the extraordinary change in budgeting and funding over the years. When we first came, the administration salary budget was just £19,000 – We had a secretary, myself, looking after the artistic leadership, administration, marketing and fund-raising, and Clare looking after all the production departments and mounting of productions. Now the theatre employs an average of fifteen people a week, in administration and production. Quite a change! The grants from public funds were virtually non-existent and it is no wonder that the organisation suffered greatly in those early years trying to get itself onto an even keel.

As I said at the start, it has been a wonderful nearly twenty-five years. Now is the time to let go, however difficult that might be. It is an opportunity for the new generation of creative leaders and I hope they will grab the opportunity and fly.

Meanwhile, I will concentrate on beating the cancer and focus on just one or two projects – rather than on the one hundred and two, as it feels like at the moment! It will be a treat not to share our home with 200 people every night and to have some privacy at the weekends, although life will seem quite quiet after the mayhem of nearly twenty-five years. And, of course, the day we turn our backs on the Watermill and drive out of the car park for the last time will be very emotional and sad, but at least we will take with us a host of happy memories, many of which I have tried to share in this little book. We will never forget our remarkable extended family, the unique Watermill family of actors, directors, writers, designers, stage managers, technicians, administrators, managers and marketeers, restaurant and bar managers, chefs, waiters waitresses and bar persons, front of house and box office staff, housekeepers, gardeners, Watermill Friends, the Watermill ducks and of course, crucially, those magnificently loyal audiences, all built up over these busy, extraordinary and very happy years.

The Final Chapter

Jill Fraser left us on the bright blue morning of February 10th 2006. But of course Jill lives on in the theatre she created with her husband James and in the memories of all, who met her, worked with her, were inspired by her and became members of that magical, fantastical community Jill referred to as her 'extended family'.

And Jill did beat the Cancer. Jill beat it because she never gave in to the illness that threatened her, always referring to her relationship with it as a 'partnership', never for a moment in public showing a shred of self-pity or defeatism. Working with Jill over the last five years since her diagnosis has been a salutary lesson to us all in the power of human courage and determination against the odds – the manifestation in life of all the values espoused for the Watermill theatre in this book. Jill never accepted that she might die; that her plans for her future retirement might not come to fruition, or that there was any alternative than to live every minute of every day to the full. Right until that last bright day in February Jill was working for her theatre, making plans, commissioning work, sketching her final extraordinary season on an enormous wall planner – excited at the prospect of a final thrilling empty year to plan, an empty calendar – a space in time to be filled with her special creations. Where was her illness in all of this? Nowhere to be seen, not in those sparkling blue eyes, so fixed on the future and all those vast possibilities.

And Jill's creations were the teams she built over the years, some of whom are detailed in these pages. It was Jill's supreme talent to see potential and to create superb groups of creative individuals able to bring that potential to the fore. So many of us will be eternally grateful for the opportunities Jill gave to us, it would be almost unthinkable in any other contemporary theatrical context to have such a loyal patron and to be allowed to grow. So many of us owe her such an enormous depth of gratitude – directors, designers, actors, musicians, technicians, stage managers, theatre and restaurant managers and administrators; Jill allowed people the creative freedom to fully become themselves, and there are precious few with that selfless talent.

As the Watermill heads into the future, how that great lady would smile to see the theatre – in many ways her first child – so long-limbed and strong now, as it walks from under her protecting wing! How proud and pleased Jill would have been to see her own family and loyal colleagues shepherding her dream so well towards new pastures.

And of course Jill still seems to be here, her in-tray is still in the office, her voice still welcomes on the answer-phone. As we walk into Jill's future, the Watermill Theatre is still Jill Fraser's special creation and I know it will always retain the hallmark of her standards, her expectation of excellence, her love for both the cutting edge and the reinvention of classics, the sound of music vibrating like the old mill stones in all that old wood. We should not worry and we should not fear – Jill never did. Whoever occupies these precious buildings with their particular magic will breathe the same air as the indefatigable Jill Fraser and be buoyed by the same unique inspiration.

One of Jill's last projects was to commission Julieann Worral Hood to design a series of permanent mosaic stepping stones leading onto the Watermill top lawn, the artwork, to be completed in 2007, will be called 'River of Dreams' and is inspired by the poem 'He wishes for the cloths of heaven' by W b Yeats. These stones will be a celebration of Jill's life, work and vision and some of the words from the poem will flow through the mosaic – just as the river Lambourn flows beneath the theatre. This will be Jill's message to the future and, as ever, her choice is fitting and to the point. Jill Fraser shared her precious dreams with us all.

Had I the heavens' embroidered cloths,
Enwrought with golden and silver light,
The blue and the dim and the dark cloths
Of night and light and the half-light,
I would spread the cloths under your feet:
But I, being poor, have only my dreams;
I have spread my dreams under your feet;
Tread softly because you tread on my dreams.

William Butler Yeats

Ade Morris July 2006

Theatre Development

1960	Judy Gollins finally acquired all the buildings on 1¾ acres of land from her estranged husband.
1960	Built the front drive – £60. Planted the front lawn and paved the area outside the mill house and beside the mill – £50
1961	Planted the back lawn – £75 Built the garden walls and back terrace – £100
1962	Built the lily pond and paved the surround – £70 Built the steps up to the barn and made the oak door – £25
1963	Replaced the west roof of the barn and lined it – £300
1964	Built low brick wall and columns and partly roofed the lily pond – £350
1965	Conversion of the mill into a theatre got underway – total estimated cost over the period until 1969 – £7,500
1968/9	Stable block converted into Watermill Cottage for actors' accommodation and providing 2 public ladies' toilets – £7,000
1972	Auditorium rebuilt to seat 170. Foyer constructed, bar, kitchen, workshops, bungalow and flat for more actors' accommodation – £20,000, including larger control box, fire escape, fire insulation and separation of bar and restaurant.
2002	Extension to the bar
2003	New cloakrooms

Appendix

1965

The Berkshire Shakespeare Players
The Taming of the Shrew (Sept 11 – 12)
Unicorn Opera Group
La Finta Giardiniera (Sept 19 – 20)

1966

The Berkshire Shakespeare Players
Twelfth Night (Jul 9 – 10)
Progress Theatre
A Man for All Seasons (Jul 23 – 24)
Unit Delta Plus
Electronic Music Concert (Sept 10)
Unicorn Opera Group
Poro (Sept 11)

1967

Peter Webster – Artistic Director
Antony Ferrand – Associate Director
Under Milk Wood by Dylan Thomas (directed by
Malcolm Taylor)
Rattle of A Simple Man (directed by Malcolm Taylor)
The Creeper (directed by Malcolm Taylor)
Night Must Fall by Emlyn Williams
The Caretaker by Harold Pinter (directed by
Antony Ferrand)
Sammy by John Mortimer
Private Lives by Noel Coward
Dock Brief by John Mortimer

1968

David Rayner – Artistic Director
Blithe Spirit by Noel Coward
Look Back in Anger by John Osborne
Victorian Music Hall
How Pleasant to Know Mr Lear by Charles Lewsen
– Premiere
The Late Edwina Black by William Morum
The Glass Menagerie by Tennessee Williams
Relatively Speaking by Alan Ayckbourn

1969

Leslie Lawton – Artistic Director
Gaslight by Patrick Hamilton (directed by Leslie Lawton)
The Flip Side by Hugh & Margaret Williams (directed by Michael Cotterill)
Ghosts by Henrik Ibsen (directed by Richard Martin)
Victorian Music Hall (directed by Roy Patrick)
On Approval by Frederick Lonsdale (directed by Guy Slater)
Who's Afraid of Virginia Woolf by Edward Albee (directed by Leslie Lawton)
The Private Ear & The Public Eye by Peter Shaffer (directed by Tania Lieven)
The Rivals by Sheridan (directed by Leslie Lawton)

1970

Nicolas Kent – Artistic Director
David Gollins – Administrator
The Grass is Greener by Hugh & Margaret Williams
La Musica & Man of Destiny by Bernard Shaw
Dance of Death – by Strindberg
Victorian Music Hall

The Milk Train Doesn't Stop Here Anymore by Tennessee Williams
Plaza Suite by Neil Simon
The Entertainer by John Osborne

1971

Peter Farago – Artistic Director
Paul Iles – General Manager
Boeing Boeing by Mark Camoletti
Next Time I'll Sing to You by James Saunders
Victorian Music Hall
The Price by Arthur Miller
Mixed Doubles
Snowdroppers by Alun Richards – Premiere
1 week of one man shows
Barefoot in the Park by Neil Simon

1972

Neil McCallum – Artistic Director
Paul Iles – General Manager
Not Now Darling by Ray Cooney & John Chapman (directed by Neil McCallum)
Ruffian on the Stairs by Joe Orton & The End of the Beginning by Sean O'Casey (directed by Frank Nesbitt)
Miss Julie by Strindberg (directed by Nicolas Kent)
Victorian Music Hall – Players' Theatre
I am Tomarienka by Alexander Coburn – Premiere (directed by Guy Slater)
The Living Room by Graham Greene (directed by Roger Jenkins)
There's A Girl In My Soup by Terence Frisby (directed by Roger Jenkins)

1973

David Gollins – Artistic Director

Paul Iles – General Manager

Two Comic Interludes by Cervantes

Leonardo's Last Supper by Peter Barnes

Getting On by Alan Bennett (directed by Philip Antony)

The Wind in the Branches of the Sassafras by Rene de Obaldia

The Daughter in Law by DH Lawrence (directed by John McKelvey)

School for Wives by Moliere (directed by Jeremy Young)

Time and Time Again by Alan Ayckbourn (directed by Brian Sheeky)

Victorian Music Hall

1974

David Gollins – Artistic Director

Paul Iles – General Manager

The Snowdroppers by Alun Richards

The Man Most Likely To by Joyce Raeburn (directed by Christopher Dunham)

A Doll's House by Henrik Ibsen (directed by Jeremy Young)

Private Lives by Noel Coward (directed by Jeremy Young)

What The Butler Saw by Joe Orton (directed by Jeremy Young)

Glasstown by Noel Robinson

Victorian Music Hall

and

Spaceship Earth – Wessex Folk Theatre

Sally Miles as The Ruined Maid

The Barrow Poets

Roy Plomley presents his own Desert Island Discs

1975

David Gollins – Artistic Director

Paul Iles – General Manager

Two and Two Make Sex by Richard Harris and Leslie Darbon

When We Dead Awaken by Henrik Ibsen (directed by Jeremy Young)

Fallen Angels by Noel Coward (directed by Jeremy Young)

Candida by George Bernard Shaw

Who Saw Him Die? by Gates

Victorian Music Hall

and

Affairs in Marriage – Kennet Theatre Company

The Magic Carpet – Polka Theatre for Children

1976

David Gilmore – Artistic Director

Canaries Sometime Sing by Frederick Lonsdale (directed by David Gilmore)

Sleuth by Anthony Shaffer (directed by David Gilmore)

Alphabetical Order by Michael Frayn

Uncle Vanya by Anton Chehov

Loot by Joe Orton

The Life & Crimes of Al Capone by Gerald Frow

and

Dido and Aeneas – The Oxford Pro Musica

The Enchanted Theatre – Polka Theatre for Children

1977

David Gilmore – Artistic Director

The Heiress by Henry James (directed by David Gilmore)

Hay Fever by Noel Coward (direceted by Peter Watson)

Butley by Simon Gray (directed by David Gilmore)

Wait Until Dark by Frederick Knott (directed by Peter Watson)

The Odd Couple by Neil Simon

Chez Nous by Peter Nichols

Victorian Music Hall

and

From Berlin to Broadway – The Oxford Pro Musica

The Feast of Lanterns – Polka Theatre for Children

1978

David Gilmore – Artistic Director

Anthony McDonald – General Manager

The Glass Menagerie by Tennessee Williams

See How They Run by Philip King

Kennedy's Children by Robert Patrick

The Bed Before Yesterday by Ben Travers

The Philanthropist by Christopher Hampton

The Great British Musical by Gilmore/Cotton

and

An Evening with Quentin Crisp

Wax Fruit – Bag and Baggage Women's Theatre Company

Kemp's Jig – Chris Harris

Songs of Love and War – The Oxford Pro Musica

1979

Michael Elwyn – Artistic Director

Anthony McDonald – General Manager

A Day in the Death of Joe Egg by Peter Nichols

Dial M for Murder by Frederick Knott

The Secretary Bird by William Douglas Home (directed by Christopher Masters)

Hedda Gabler by Henrik Ibsen (directed by Michael Elwyn)

Absent Friends by Alan Ayckbourn

Otherwise Engaged by Simon Gray
The Hollow Crown devised by John Barton
and
The World of Gilbert and Sullivan – The Young Savoyards
The Magic of the Lantern – Whites Wonders

1980

Michael Elwyn – Artistic Director
Judith Dixey – General Manager
Can You Hear Me at the Back? by Brian Clark
Clouds by Michael Frayn
Move Over Mrs Markham by Ray Cooney & John Chapman
Mrs Warren's Profession by George Bernard Shaw
Abigail's Party by Mike Leigh
Tishoo by Brian Thompson
Side by Side by Sondheim
and
Bottom's Dream – puppets
Songs from the Garden – singers from the Royal Opera
House Covent Garden
The World of Rodgers and Hammerstein – The Young
Savoyards
English Woodwind Quartet
A Gala Evening with Ian Wallace
Toni Arthur's Music Box

1981

Michael Elwyn – Artistic Director
Judith Dixey – General Manager
Entertaining Mr Sloane by Joe Orton
Last of the Red Hot Lovers by Neil Simon (directed by
John Doyle)
The Old Country by Alan Bennett (directed by
Michael Elwyn)

Just Between Ourselves by Alan Ayckbourn (directed by John Doyle)

Rosmersholm by Henrik Ibsen (directed by Michael Elwyn)

Night & Day by Tom Stoppard (directed by Michael Elwyn)

Bodies by James Saunders (directed by John Doyle)

The Gingerbread Man by David Wood (directed by Wendy Toye)

and

Canterbury Tales – Jill Freud & Company

Instant Sunshine

Twisted Cues and Elliptical Balls – John Judd

I Say, I play – Jennie Linden and Janet Edwards

Annie Ross with the Harry South Quartet

1982

Jill Fraser – Artistic Director /Executive Director

Duet for One by Tom Kempinski (directed by Philip Grout)

Twelfth Night by William Shakespeare (directed by Euan Smith)

Stage Struck by Simon Gray (directed by Mark Woolgar)

The Killing of Sister George by Frank Marcus (directed by Patrick Lau)

Outside Edge by Richard Harris (directed by Patrick Lau)

This Thing Called Love by Alec Grahame, David Kernan, John Moffat – Premiere (directed by Wendy Toye)

Christmas Cat and the Pudding Pirates by Jeanette Ranger and Christopher Lillicrap – Premiere (directed by Peter Clough)

Visiting artists

Old Herbaceous by Alfred Shaugnessy with Roger Hume

The Bird Man/Monkey Tricks/The Ancient Mariner – Moving Stage Marionettes (Saturday children's show)

The Cambridge Buskers (Sunday night)

The Great Kovari's Magic Show (Saturday children's show)

Pete Allen Jazz Band (Sunday lunch)

The Echoing Green with Richard Pasco and Barbara Leigh Hunt (Sunday night)

Steafel Solo with Sheila Steafel (Sunday night)

Toni Arthur's Music Box (Saturday children's show)

The Swing Guitars (Sunday lunch)

English Songs with Kathleen Livingstone (Sunday night)

Jonathan Cohen's Music Workshop (Saturday children's show)

Keith James and Toffs (Sunday lunch)

Zippo the Clown (Saturday children's show)

An Evening of Louis Armstrong & Fats Waller – George Chisholm and Keith Smith's Hefty Jazz (Sunday night)

Victorian Music Hall – Players' Theatre

Judi Dench & Michael Williams (Sunday night)

The Paper Town Paper Chase by David Wood – Caricature Theatre (Children's show)

1983

Romeo and Juliet by William Shakespeare (directed by Euan Smith)

Table Manners by Alan Ayckbourn (directed by Euan Smith)

The Fourposter by Jan de Hartog (directed by Philip Grout)

Snoopy by Charles M Schultz, Warren Lockhart, Arthur Whitelaw and Michael L Grace with music by Larry Grossman and lyrics by Hal Hackady (directed by Arthur Whitelaw)

Old Time Music Hall – Players' Theatre

Monty Moonbeam's Magnificent Mission by Jeanette Ranger and Christopher Lillicrap – Premiere (directed by Peter Clough)

Visiting artists

Julie Felix (Sunday night)
Wayland Smithy (Sunday lunch)
Mr Acker Bilk and his Paramount Jazz Band (Sunday night)
Brian Cant's Fun Book (Saturday children's show)
Robert Tear (Sunday night)
Toni Arthur's Music Box (Saturday children's show)
Keith James in Concert (Sunday night)
David Whetstone & Jean Pierre Rasle (Sunday lunch)
The Yetties (Sunday night)
Bo's Travelling Circus (Saturday children's show)
Common Thyme (Sunday lunch)
Two Inches of Ivory with Geraldine McEwan (Sunday night)
The Pete Allen Jazz Band (Sunday lunch)
Jacolly Puppets (Saturday children's show)
The New Dixie Six (Sunday night)
The Ray Shields Orchestra and Singers (Sunday night)
An Evening with Donald Swann at the Piano (Sunday night)

1984

The Merchant of Venice by William Shakespeare (directed by Pip Broughton)
Woodworm by Fay Weldon – Premiere (directed by Paul Unwin)
The Man Most Likely To by Joyce Raeburn (directed by Christopher G Sandford)
Noel & Gertie by Sheridan Morley (directed by Wendy Toye)
September in the Rain by John Godber (directed by John Godber)
Old Herbaceous by Alfred Shaugnessy with Roger Hume
Pinocchio by Euan Smith with music by Peter Murray – Premiere (directed by Christopher G Sandford)

*CLANDESTINE
MARRIAGE*
(2001)
L to R: Sam
Dastor (Lord
Ogleby), Jane
Cameron
(Fanny), Clare
McCarron (Miss
Sterling), Helen
Murton (Betty).
*Photo: Laurence
Burns.*

LOVE IN A MAZE (2002)
L to R: Cate Debenham Taylor (Mrs Lucy Buckethorne), Martin
Hutson (Colonel Rupert Buckethorne), Nick Caldecott (Lord Minever),
Sam Dastor (Sir Able Buckethorne), Robert Benfield (Sir Toby
Nettletop), Eileen Battye (Lady Aurora Fullalove), Claire Carrie (Faith),
Paul Harvard (Mopus). *Photo: Laurence Burns.*

Sir Michael Hordern, Chairman of the Friends of the Watermill.

THE KILLING OF SISTER GEORGE (1982)
Peggy Mount (Sister George).
Photo: Laurence Burns.

The Restaurant.
Photo: Laurence Burns.

The Bar
Photo: Laurence Burns.

THE MERCHANT OF VENICE in Pakistan (1984)
L to R: ?, Alan White, Mark Knox, Jack Galloway, Gavin Muir, ?,
President of Pakistan-Muhammad Zia-ul-Haq, Bernard Kay, Med
Davies, ?, Kathryn Hunter, Celia Imrie, Crispin Redman, British
Council Representative.
Photo: Clare Lindsay.

THE WINTER'S TALE Propeller in San Francisco (2005)
L to R: Heather Davies (Assistant Director), Bob Barrett, Chris Myles,
Jamie Beamish, William Buckhurst, Vince Leigh, Alasdair Craig.

A MIDSUMMER NIGHT'S DREAM (2003)
L to R: Vince Leigh (Snout), Jules Werner (Flute), Simon Scardifield
(Starveling), Chris Myles (Quince), Jonathan McGuinness (Snug).
Photo: Laurence Burns.

THE WINTER'S TALE (2005)
L to R: Richard Clothier, Adam Levy, Tam Williams (Perdita), Chris
Myles (Old Shepherd), Tony Bell (Autolycus), Bob Barrett (Camillo),
Vince Leigh (Polixenes), Alisdair Craig, James Tucker (Young
Shepherd), Jules Werner (Mopsa).
Photo: Alastair Muir.

OUTREACH PRODUCTIONS

Left: *THE DREAMER* (2000)
L to R: Glyn Dilley, Clara Onyemere and Christopher Tajah (Martin)
Photo: Philip Tull

Below: *GIGOLO* (2003)
L to R: Glyn Dilley (Mike) and Andrew Cryer (Paul).
Photo: Philip Tull

I DREAMT I DWELT IN MARBLE HALLS (2002)
L to R: Shaun Hennessy (George), Ann Marcuson (Madelyn), Matthew Morrison (Daniel/Liam).
Photo: Philip Tull

SWEENEY TODD (1987)
Neil McCaul (Sweeney Todd) and
Charles Millham (Judge).

SWEENEY TODD (1987) Neil
McCaul (Sweeney Todd) and
Lesley Duff (Mrs Lovett).

SWEENEY TODD (2004)
Paul Hegarty (Sweeney Todd) and
Michael Howcroft (Beadle)

SWEENEY TODD (2004)
Paul Hegarty (Sweeney Todd) and
Karen Mann (Mrs Lovett)

Photographs: Laurence Burns

JUST SO (1989)
L to R: Erick Ray Evans (Parsee), Okon Jones (Ethipian), Paul Gyngell (Leopard), Dawn Spence (Giraffe), Simon Bowman (Kangeroo), Charles Millham (Rhino), Julie Armstrong (Zebra), Sally Anne Triplett (Kola Kola Bird). foreground: Anthony Barclay (Elephant Child) background: Martin Smith (Kipling & Eldest Magician).
Photo: Michael Le Poer Trench copyright Cameron Mackintosh Ltd.

THE CARD (1992)
L to R: Peter Duncan (Denry), David Alder (Shillitoe), Matthew White (Parsloe), Jacintha White (Nellie).
Photo: Michael Le Poer Trench copyright Cameron Mackintosh Ltd.

Jill with Cameron Mackintosh (1992).
Photo: Laurence Burns.

ABOVE: *THE UGLY DUCKLING* (1993), Alison Jiear (Ida).
Photo: Laurence Burns

BELOW: *WARTS AND ALL* (1996). L to R: George Stiles, Jenna Russell,
Anthony Drewe, Alison Jiear, Aled Jones.
Photo: Laurence Burns

CABARET (1998)
Jo Baird (Sally Bowles) with Mike Afford
Photo: Laurence Burns

The By-pass Protests (1995/1996)

CHARLOTTE'S WEB (1995)
The understudies – Jill (Goose) and Jan Doyle (Martha)
Photo: Peter Bloodworth.

BLOOD BROTHERS (1986)
L to R: Lesley Rooney (Mrs Lyons) and Louise Gold (Mrs Johnstone)
Photo: Conrad Blakemore.

Jill awarded the MBE by the Queen in 2005 for her services to drama
The family on their return from the Palace
Photo: Clare Lindsay

'The Jill Fraser Memorial Garden'
donated to the Watermill by the Friends of the Watermill
Photo: Rosemary Haynes

Visiting artists

TVS Showcase series with Nigel Kennedy, Soft Touch, Sarah Brightman

Façade – Berkshire 20th Century Music Group (Saturday children's show)

George Melly & John Chilton's Feetwarmers (Sunday night)

Rolo & Shandy (Saturday children's show)

Musical Mystery Tour (Saturday children's show)

An Evening of Bull with Peter Bull

A Week of A Summer Soufflé:

Take a Sparkling Pair with Peter Pratt and friends

Steafel Lately with Sheila Steafel

The Medici String Quartet

How Pleasant to Know Mr Lear with Nicholas Parsons

An Evening in the company of Bernard Miles and Josephine Wilson

A Portrait of Fryderyk Chopin with Nelly Ben-Or and Gabrielle Woolf

Pete Sayers in Concert (Sunday night)

Marian Montgomery & Richard Rodney Bennett (Sunday night)

Bother! An Hour with Pooh. Or More. Bother! (Saturday children's show)

The Temperance Seven (Sunday night)

Captain Pugwash (Saturday children's show)

A Funny Kind of Evening with David Kossoff

Lucky Bag with Victoria Wood

Common Lore

Clara Clarissima with Felicity Lott and Gabriel Woolf

1985

What the Eye Can't See by George Feydeau (directed by Christopher G Sandford)

In Praise of Love by Terence Rattigan (directed by Celia Bannerman)

The Archers by William Smethurst – Premiere (directed by Patrick Tucker)

How the Other Half Loves by Alan Ayckbourn (directed by Brian Stirner)

Once Upon A Mattress by Mary Rogers, Marshall Barer, Jay Thompson & Dean Fuller (directed by Wendy Toye)

Sleuth by Anthony Shaffer (directed by Alison Sutcliffe)

Jack & the Beanstalk by Euan Smith – Premiere (directed by Patrick Tucker)

Visiting Artists

This Day's Delight with Edward Woodward & Michelle Dotrice (Sunday night)

Sunday Lunchtime Jazz with The Pete Allen Jazz Band

Kovari's Magic Show (Saturday children's show)

The Great Soprendo's Mystery Show (Sunday night)

Think of a Number with Johnny Ball (Saturday children's show)

Cantabile – Barbershop Quartet (Sunday night)

Zippo and Company (Saturday children's show)

Galaxy of Song with John Boulter and John Lawrenson (Sunday night)

Kenny Ball and His Jazzmen (Sunday night)

Christopher Lillicrap (Saturday children's show)

Jazzin' Around with the Pete Allen Jazz Band (Sunday night)

1986

The Importance of Being Earnest by Oscar Wilde (directed by Christopher G Sandford)

The Real Thing by Tom Stoppard (directed by Christopher G Sandford)

A Killing Time by Euan Smith – Premiere (directed by Nick Philippou)

Blood Brothers by Willy Russell (directed by Ceri Sherlock)

The Owl and the Pussycat by Bill Manhoff (directed by Maria Charles)

Beauty and the Beast by Euan Smith with music and lyrics by Peter Murray – Premiere (directed by Celia Bannerman)

Visiting Artists

Jazzin' Around with the Pete Allen Jazz Band (Sunday night)

The Mike Amatt Show (Saturday children's show)

Advice…and how not to take it with Jill Bennett and Edward Hardwicke (Sunday night)

Lucie Skeaping's Musical Mystery Tour (Saturday children's show)

Chris Barber's Jazz and Blues Band (Sunday night)

The David Wood Magic and Music Show (Saturday children's show)

The Glory of the Garden with Hannah Gordon, Martin Jenkins and Martin Best (Sunday night)

Storytelling and A Funny Kind of Evening with David Kossoff (Sunday night)

Under Milk Wood – Jill Freud and Company

Ghost Train – Newbury Dramatic Society

A Christmas Concert – The Hart Male Voice Choir

1987

Bugsy Malone – school children from Kennet, Shaw, St Barts, The Downs

Blithe Spirit by Noel Coward (directed by Christopher G Sandford)

Benefactors by Michael Frayn (directed by Christopher G Sandford)

The Winter's Tale by William Shakespeare (directed by Ceri Sherlock)

Sweeney Todd by Stephen Sondheim (directed by Timothy Prager, associate director Ceri Sherlock)

Educating Rita by Willy Russell (directed by Euan Smith)

Music Hall with Miss Helen Watson

The Quest for the Rose and the Ring by Euan Smith with music and lyrics by Peter Murray – Premiere (directed by Graham Callan)

Visiting Artists

The Pete Allen Jazz Band (Sunday lunchtimes)

Round the World in Search of Steam with Colin Garrett (Sunday night)

The Christopher Lillicrap Show (Saturday children's show)

Rockin'in Rhythm with Terry Lightfoot and his Band (Sunday night)

Common Lore (Sunday Night)

Just Like You and Me with Johnny Morris

Easy to Sing with Elizabeth Seal and Julian Slade

Children's Theatre Workshop with Peter Murray

Jazz Workshop with the Pete Allen Band

Non-Stop Jazz Day

Arms and the Man – Jill Freud and Company

See How They Run – Newbury Dramatic Society

Maureen Lipman Solo (Sunday night)

Steafel Variations with Sheila Steafel (Sunday night)

1988

Wind Among the Pines – (a musical drama written and performed by the WYT directed by Peter Murray)

Private Lives by Noel Coward (directed by Graham Callan)

Songbook by Monty Norman and Julian More (directed by Wendy Toye)

My Wife Whatsername by Christopher Lillicrap and Jonathan Izard (directed by Christopher G Sandford)

Zack by Harold Brighouse (directed by Euan Smith)
Painting Churches by Tina Howe – Premiere (directed by Mervyn Willis)
Music Hall with Miss Helen Watson
King Rollo's Stolen Christmas by Euan Smith with Graham Callan with music and lyrics by Peter Murray – Premiere (directed by Graham Callan)

Visiting Artists

The Pete Allen Jazz Band (Sunday lunchtimes)
The Mike Amatt Mop & Smiff Show (Saturday children's show)
Saturdays On Stage with Peter Murray (Saturday children's show)
The Jonathan Cohen Music Show (Saturday children's show)
She Stoops To Conquer – Jill Freud and Company

1989

Never Look Back by Peter Murray (directed by Peter Murray with the WYT)
Pack of Lies by Hugh Whitemore (directed by Graham Callan)
Just So by George Stiles and Anthony Drewe (directed by Julia McKenzie)
I Wish I Wish by Terence Brady and Charlotte Bingham – Premiere (directed by Graham Callan)
Caste by TW Robertson (directed by Euan Smith)
84 Charing Cross Road by Helen Hanff (directed by Euan Smith)
Old Herbaceous by Alfred Shaugnessy with Roger Hume
Old Time Music Hall with Miss Helen Watson
King Rollo Space Crusader by Euan Smith with music and lyrics by Peter Murray – Premiere (directed by Chris White)

Visiting Artists

The Pete Allen Jazz Band (Sunday lunchtimes)
The Great Kovari's Magic Show (Saturday children's show)
Puppet Magic with Stephen Mottram (Saturday children's show)
The David Wood Music and Magic Show (Saturday children's show)
Pete Allen's Jazz Parade (Sunday night)

1990

Our Day Out (directed by Peter Murray with the WYT)
Gaslight by Patrick Hamilton (directed by Paul Clayton)
Hand Over Fist by Richard Everett – Premiere (directed by Christopher Villiers)
The Lost Domain by Euan Smith based on the novel Le Grand Meaulnes by Alain Fournier – Premiere (directed by Chris White and Euan Smith)
Relatively Speaking by Alan Ayckbourn (directed by Graham Callan)
Moll Flanders by Claire Luckham with new music by George Stiles and additional lyrics by Paul Leigh (directed by Wendy Toye)
Ghosts by Henrik Ibsen (directed by Euan Smith)
Old Time Music Hall with Miss Helen Watson
Toad of Toad Hall by AA Milne from the book by Kenneth Grahame (directed by Paul Clayton)

Visiting Artists

The Pete Allen Jazz Band (Sunday lunchtimes)
Tales From the Forest with The All Electric Puppet Theatre (Saturday children's show)
Lucy Skeaping's Musical Mystery Tour (Saturday children's shows)

1991

Fool's Errand by Peter Murray (directed by Peter Murray with the WYT)

Good Morning Bill by P G Wodehouse (directed by Paul Clayton)

An Inspector Calls by J B Priestley (directed by Euan Smith) – the first show to be played in the round

Cold Comfort Farm by Paul Doust from the novel by Stella Gibbon – Premiere (directed by Amanda Knott)

Stepping Out by Richard Harris (directed by David Kelsey)

The Drummer or The Haunted House by Joseph Addison (directed by Wendy Toye)

Teechers by John Godber (directed by Peter Murray with the WYT)

Miss Helen Watson's Old Time Music Hall

The Wizard of Oz by L Frank Baum (directed by Euan Smith)

Visiting Artists

The Pete Allen Jazz Band (Sunday lunchtimes)

Alexandra Kollontai with Barbara Ewing (Sunday night)

Animal Farm (directed by Graham Callan with students from the Newbury College Performing Arts Course)

Jazzin' Around with the Pete Allen Jazz Band and Clinton Ford

Outside Edge – Newbury Dramatic Society

Captain Crab and the Pirates with the All Electric Puppet Theatre (Saturday children's show)

1992

25th Anniversary season

Half a Sixpence by David Heneker and Beverley Cross (directed by Peter Murray with the WYT)

See How They Run by Philip King (directed by Wendy Toye)

Hindsight by Richard Everett (directed by Euan Smith)

The Deep Blue Sea by Terence Rattigan (directed by Euan Smith)

The Card by Keith Waterhouse, Willis Hall, Tony Hatch & Jackie Trent with additional lyrics by Anthony Drewe (directed by Jeremy Sams)

Macbeth by William Shakespeare (directed by Euan Smith)

The Crucifer of Blood by Paul Giovanni (directed by Graham Callan)

Miss Helen Watson's Old Time Music Hall

Christmas Cat and the Pudding Pirates by Christopher Lillicrap and Jeanette Ranger (directed by Paul Clayton)

Visiting Artists

The Pete Allen Jazz Band (Sunday lunchtimes)

Charley's Aunt – Newbury Dramatic Society

1993

Amphibious Spangulatos! Newt on Your Nelly! by Paul Doust – Premiere (directed by Peter Murray with the WYT)

On Approval by Frederick Lonsdale (directed by Paul Clayton)

My Children! My Africa! by Athol Fugard (directed by Alby James)

The Lusty and Comical History of Tom Jones by John Morrison (directed by John Doyle)

Say Who You Are by Keith Waterhouse and Willis Hall (directed by Robin Midgley)

The Great Big Radio Show by Philip Glassborow and Nick McIvor – Premiere (directed by Angela Hardcastle)

Toys in the Attic by Lillian Hellman (directed by Euan Smith)

Old Herbaceous by Alfred Shaugnessy with Roger Hume

Miss Helen Watson's Music Hall

The Ugly Duckling by George Stiles and Anthony Drewe
– Premiere (directed by Stephen Dexter)

Visiting Artists

The Pete Allen Jazz Band (Sunday lunchtimes)
Murder at the Mill devised by Paul Clayton and Brian Jordan
(Sunday Night)
Season's Greetings – Newbury Dramatic Society

1994

Epsom Downs by Howard Brenton (directed by Trevelyan
Wright with the WYT)
What Every Woman Knows by J M Barrie (directed by
Dilys Hamlett)
Shirley Valentine by Willy Russell (directed by Stephen
Rayne)
Dilemma for Murder by Brian Jordan with Paul Clayton
– Premiere (directed by Paul Clayton)
Sticky Wickets by Paul Doust – Premiere (directed by
Paul Clayton)
The Anastasia File by Royce Ryton (directed by
Wendy Toye)
Rosmersholm by Henrik Ibsen (directed by Euan Smith)
Frankenstein by Mary Shelley (directed by Trevelyan
Wright with the WYT)
Miss Helen Watson's Music Hall
*The Secret Garden by Diana Morgan with music by Steven
Markwick* (directed by Ian Talbot)

Visiting Artists

The Pete Allen Jazz Band (Sunday lunchtimes)
Blithe Spirit – Newbury Dramatic Society

1995

Goodbye Mr Chips by Norman Coates – Premiere (directed by Angie Langfield)

The Lemon Conspiracy by Brian Jordan (directed by Julia Dickinson and Trevelyan Wright with the WYT and Sixth Sense Theatre Trust)

Thark by Ben Travers (directed by David Conville)

Tess of the d'Urbervilles adapted by Michael Fry (directed by Dilys Hamlett)

Living Together by Alan Ayckbourn (directed by Euan Smith)

Laura by Michael Heath – Premiere (directed by Charles Sharman-Cox)

Lloyd George Knew My Father by William Douglas-Home (directed by Wendy Toye)

Othello by William Shakespeare (directed by Edward Hall)

The Man Who Was Thursday by G K Chesterton (directed by Trevelyan Wright with the WYT)

Miss Helen Watson's Music Hall

Charlotte's Web by E B White, book by Joseph Robinette with music and lyrics by Charles Strouse – (directed by Dilys Hamlett)

Visiting Artists

The Pete Allen Jazz Band (Sunday lunchtimes)

I'll Get My Man by Philip King – Newbury Dramatic Society

1996

Warts & All by George Stiles and Anthony Drewe – Premiere (directed by Wendy Toye)

The Adding Machine by Elmer Rice (directed by Trevelyan Wright with the WYT)

Driving Miss Daisy by Alfred Uhry (directed by David Massarella)

The Entertainer by John Osborne (directed by Stephen Rayne)

Round and Round the Garden by Alan Ayckbourn (directed by Euan Smith)

Rogues to Riches book & lyrics by Robert Sevra, music by Lynn Crigler – British Premiere (directed by Wendy Toye)

Couch Grass & Ribbon by Adam Thorpe – Premiere (directed by Kate Beales)

Lettice & Lovage by Peter Shaffer (directed by Dilys Hamlett)

The Wedding Party by David Sulkin with music by Karen Wimhurst (directed by Trevelyn Wright with the WYT, West Berkshire Music Centre and the Corn Exchange)

Miss Helen Watson's Music Hall

Peter Pan adapted by Philip Glassborow – Premiere (directed by Dilys Hamlett)

Visiting Artists

Midsummer Jazz Barbecue featuring The Pete Allen Jazz Band (Sunday night)

Bluebeard's Castle – Theatre du Sygne & Noise Inc. (Tokyo)

Hamlet – Premiere – Kaboodle Productions

Flying Feathers – Newbury Dramatic Society

1997

Mixed Doubles by Alan Ayckbourn, John Bowen, Lyndon Brook, David Campton, Alun Owen, Harold Pinter and James Saunders (directed by Graham Callan)

The Green of the Spring by Ade Morris – Premiere (directed by Ade Morris with the West Berkshire Federation of Village Schools)

Bullets & Beetroot Lips by Ade Morris – Premiere (directed by Ade Morris with the WYT)

Deadwood – A Soldier Returns by Alex Jones – Premiere (directed by Stephen Rayne)

Henry V by William Shakespeare – Propeller (directed by Edward Hall)

30 Not Out – a celebration of 30 years of the Watermill (directed by Wendy Toye)

Table Manners by Alan Ayckbourn (directed by Euan Smith)

Live Radio Theatre Project – rehearsed readings in the studio

Little Shop of Horrors book & lyrics by Howard Ashman with music by Alan Menken (directed by Martin Connor)

Far From the Madding Crowd by Thomas Hardy adapted by Matthew White (directed by Matthew White)

Wait Until Dark by Frederick Knott (directed by Euan Smith)

How to be a Monster by Ade Morris – Premiere (directed by Ade Morris with the WYT)

Miss Helen Watson's Music Hall

The Adventures of Mr Toad – book, music and lyrics by Piers Chater-Robinson (directed by Dilys Hamlett)

Visiting Artists

La Bohème – with Camberwell Pocket Opera

Scouting for Boys with The Stennett Company

Our Country's Good by Timberlake Wertenbaker – Box Theatre Company

Midday Jazz Buffet with The Pete Allen Jazz Band

The Pete Allen Jazz Band (Sunday night)

Move Over Mrs Markham – Newbury Dramatic Society

1998

Talking Heads by Alan Bennett (directed by Euan Smith)

Flying by Ade Morris – Premiere (directed by Ade Morris with the WYT)

Snoopy by Charles M Schultz, Warren Lockhart, Arthur Whitelaw and Michael L Grace with music by Larry Grossman and lyrics by Hal Hackady (directed by Anthony Drewe)

The Salmon's Tale by Ade Morris – Premiere – Outreach Schools' Tour (directed by Ade Morris)

The Comedy of Errors by William Shakespeare – Propeller (directed by Edward Hall)

Henry V by William Shakespeare – Propeller (directed by Edward Hall)

Absurd Person Singular by Alan Ayckbourn (directed by Euan Smith)

Cabaret – book by Joe Masteroff with music by John Kander and lyrics by Fred Ebb (directed by John Doyle)

The Government Inspector by Nikolai Gogol adapted by Philip Goulding (directed by Stephen Rayne)

Skylight by David Hare (directed by Euan Smith)

You Make Me Happy When Skies Are Grey by Ade Morris – Premiere (directed by Ade Morris with the WYT)

Comedy Music Hall with Miss Helen Watson

The Wizard of Oz by L Frank Baum (directed and staged by John Doyle)

Visiting Artists

Habeus Corpus – Newbury Dramatic Society

1999

More Talking Heads by Alan Bennett (directed by Euan Smith)

Green Man by Ade Morris – Premiere (directed by Ade Morris with the West Berkshire Federation of Village Schools)

The Salmon's Tale by Ade Morris – Outreach schools' tour (directed by Ade Morris)

Dracula by Liz Lochhead (directed by Ade Morris with the WYT)

Dangerous Corner by J B Priestley (directed by Guy Retallack)

Twelfth Night by William Shakespeare – Propeller (directed by Edward Hall)

Woman in Mind by Alan Ayckbourn (directed by Euan Smith)

Irma La Douce – English book & lyrics by Julian More, David Heneker and Monty Norman with music by Margueritte Monnot (directed by John Doyle)

Death and the Maiden by Ariel Dorfman (directed by Euan Smith)

A Little of What You Fancy with Miss Helen Watson

The Mill on the Floss by George Elliot adapted by Helen Edmundson (directed by Ade Morris with the Young Company)

Sinbad by Christopher Lillicrap (directed by John Doyle)

Visiting Artists

The Bridge by Alex Jones – Pentabus Theatre Company

2000

Travels with my Aunt by Graham Greene (directed by Euan Smith)

The Dreamer by Ade Morris – Premiere (directed by Ade Morris)

Lord of the Flies by William Golding adapted by Nigel Williams (directed by Ade Morris with the WYT)

Hard Times by Charles Dickens adapted by Stephen Jeffreys (directed by Guy Retallack)

Green Man by Ade Morris (directed by Steve Johnstone with the Kennet Federation of Village Schools)

Up 'n' Under by John Godber (directed by Robert Horwell)

Carmen adapted by John Doyle (directed by John Doyle)

The Well in the Wood – The Boxford Masques adapted by Geraldine McCaughrean – Boxford community play (directed by Ade Morris)

Old World by Aleksei Arbuzov translated by Ariadne Nicolaeff (directed by Euan Smith)
The Prisoner of Zenda by Anthony Hope adapted by Euan Smith (directed by Robert Horwell)
A Little More of What You Fancy with Miss Helen Watson
Dragon's Teeth by Peter Cann (directed by Ade Morris with the Young Company)
Beauty and the Beast adapted by John Doyle (directed by John Doyle)

2001

Rose Rage by William Shakespeare – Propeller – Premiere (directed by Edward Hall)
Lone Flyer by Ade Morris – Premiere (directed by Ade Morris)
The Gondoliers adapted by John Doyle (directed by John Doyle)
Carmen adapted by John Doyle (directed by John Doyle)
The Importance of Being Earnest by Oscar Wilde (directed by Matthew Smith)
Walk in the Shadow by Ben Myers – Premiere (directed by Ben Myers with the WYT)
Clandestine Marriage by George Coleman & David Garrick (directed by Timothy Sheader)
Witch by Ade Morris – Premiere (directed by Ade Morris with the Young Company)
Even More of What You Fancy with Miss Helen Watson
Piaf by Pam Gems (directed by John Doyle)
Cinderella and the Enchanted Slipper by John Doyle – Premiere (directed by John Doyle)

Visiting Artists

The Merchant of Venice – Theatre du Sygne (Tokyo)

2002

Fen by Caryl Churchill (directed by Ade Morris with the Young Company)

Only A Matter of Time by Alan Plater – Premiere (directed by John Doyle)

I Dreamt I Dwelt in Marble Halls by Ade Morris – Premiere (directed by Ade Morris)

Fiddler on the Roof book by Joseph Stein, music by Jerry Bock, lyrics by Sheldon Harnick (directed by John Doyle)

Love in a Maze by Dion Boucicault (directed by Timothy Sheader)

Beth the Bin Lady by Ade Morris – Premiere – Outreach Schools' Tour (directed by Ade Morris)

Dancing at Lughnasa by Brian Friel (directed by Jonathan Munby)

Ten Cents A Dance – the music and lyrics of Rogers and Hart – Premiere (conceived and directed by John Doyle)

Miss Helen Watson's Seasonal Sauce

Landmines and Chewing Gum by Ben Myers – Premiere (directed by Ben Myers with the WYT)

The Firebird by Neil Duffield (directed by Robert Horwell)

Visiting Artists

The Crucible – Newbury Dramatic Society

A Doll's House – Box Theatre Company

2003

A Midsummer Night's Dream by William Shakespeare – Propeller (directed by Edward Hall)

Gigolo by Ade Morris – Premiere (directed by Ade Morris)

Raising Voices – Glass Eels, That Good Night, Chasing Dreams, Land of the Midday Night, Last Summer, The Fourth Fold – 6 rehearsed readings of new writing

The Triumph of Love by Pierre Carlet de Marivaux translated by Martin Crimp (directed by Jonathan Munby)

Accelerate by Ade Morris – Premiere (directed by Ade Morris with the Young Company)

Call to the Sky by Ade Morris – Premiere (directed by Will Wollen with the West Berkshire Federation of Village Schools)

Dreams from a Summerhouse by Alan Ayckbourn with music by John Pattison (directed by Timothy Sheader)

The Last Days of the Empire by Alan Plater with music by John Dankworth – Premiere (directed by John Doyle)

The Fourth Fold by Gavin Rogers – Premiere (directed by Will Wollen)

A Star Danced by John Doyle with music by Sarah Travis – Premiere (directed by John Doyle)

Wallride by Ben Myers with music by Phil White – Premiere (directed by Ben Myers with the WYT)

Seasonal Sauce with Miss Helen Watson

The Emperor and the Nightingale by Neil Duffield with music by Paul Kissaun (directed by Fiona Laird)

Visiting Artists

Rising Stars Concert

An Ideal Husband – Newbury Dramatic Society

2004

Sweeney Todd with book by Hugh Wheeler and music and lyrics by Stephen Sondheim (directed and designed by John Doyle)

Mr & Mrs Schultz by Alex Jones – Premiere (directed by Ade Morris)

The Gentleman from Olmedo by Lope de Vega translated by David Johnston (directed by Jonathan Munby)

The Venetian Twins by Carlo Goldoni translated by Ranjit Bolt (directed by Jonathan Munby)

Hope Springs by Richard Conlan (directed by Ben Myers with the WYT)

The Seven Stars – The Boxford Masques adapted by Geraldine McCaughrean – Boxford community play (directed by Ade Morris)

Pinafore Swing adapted by John Doyle with musical arrangements by Sarah Travis – Premiere (directed by John Doyle)

Raising Voices – The Weatherman's Harvest, Bringing up Baby, A Conspiracy of Furniture, Harmony, Chalk and Cheese – 5 rehearsed readings of new writing

The Comedian by Ade Morris – Premiere (directed by Ade Morris)

Neville's Island by Tim Firth (directed by Heather Davies)

Multiplex by Christopher William Hill – (Directed by Ade Morris with the Young Company)

Seasonal Sauce with Miss Helen Watson

Arabian Nights by Neil Duffield (directed by Andy Brereton)

Visiting Artists

Three Men in a Boat – Rodney Bewes

Rising Stars

Whose Life Is It Anyway by Brian Clark – Newbury Dramatic Society

2005

The Winter's Tale by William Shakespeare – Propeller (directed by Edward Hall)

The Comedian by Ade Morris (directed by Ade Morris)

Broken Glass by Arthur Miller (directed by Andy Brereton)

The Odyssey adapted by Will Wollen – Premiere (directed by Will Wollen with the WYT)

Mack and Mabel by Jerry Herman, Michael Stewart and Francine Pascal (directed by John Doyle)

The Shed by Ade Morris – Premiere (directed by Will Wollen with the West Berkshire Federation of Village Schools)

Thieves' Carnival by Jean Anouilh translated by Lucienne Hill (directed by Andy Brereton)
The Garden at Llangoed by Ade Morris – Premiere (directed by Ade Morris)
Copenhagen by Michael Frayn (directed by Heather Davies)
The Gilded Lilies by Ade Morris (directed by Ade Morris with the Young Company)
Miss Helen Watson's Seasonal Sauce
The Jungle Book by Neil Duffield (directed by Andy Brereton)

Visiting Artists

A Streetcar Named Desire by Tennessee Williams – Box Theatre Company
Summer Sauce Garden Party
Racing Demon by David Hare – Newbury Dramatic Society

2006

Tartuffe by Molière translated and adapted by Ranjit Bolt (directed by Jonathan Munby)

OVERSEAS TOURING

1983

ROMEO & JULIET
Sweden

1984

THE MERCHANT OF VENICE
India, Pakistan, Sri Lanka, Nepal, Iraq

1986

THE REAL THING
Cyprus, Egypt, Israel, Turkey

1987

EDUCATING RITA

Brazil

1992

MACBETH

Japan, Argentina

1995

LIVING TOGETHER

Malta

OTHELLO

Japan

1997

HENRY V

Germany

1998

THE COMEDY OF ERRORS & HENRY V

Cyprus, Malta, Germany, Italy, Mexico, Bangladesh, Sri
Lanka, Indonesia, Malaysia, the Philippines

2000

CARMEN

Cyprus

2001

ROSE RAGE

Eire, Italy

2002

ROSE RAGE

Turkey, Poland

2003

A MIDSUMMER NIGHT'S DREAM

Barbados, Germany, Italy

2004

A MIDSUMMER NIGHT'S DREAM
USA (Brooklyn, New York)

2005

THE WINTER'S TALE
Germany, Eire, Spain (Madrid, Girona), USA (Brooklyn, San Francisco, Washington)

UK TOURING

1994

ANASTASIA & ROSMERSHOLM
Epsom

1995

GOODBYE MR CHIPS
Poole, Bracknell, Taunton, Bury St Edmunds, Lincoln, Harlow, Huddersfield

TESS OF THE D'URBERVILLES
Cheltenham

1996

THE ENTERTAINER
Cheltenham, London (Hampstead)

1997

FAR FROM THE MADDING CROWD
Coventry

1998

HENRY V & THE COMEDY OF ERRORS
London (Pleasance), Bowness on Windermere, Stratford upon Avon (+ overseas)

THE SALMON'S TALE (Tour 1)
Theale, Greenham, Chaddleworth St Andrews, Hermitage, Newbury, Thatcham, Hungerford,

Aldermaston, Inkpen, Shaw, Enborne, Shefford, Bucklebury, East Woodhay, Chieveley, Stockcross, Welford, Wickham

1999

THE SALMON'S TALE (Tour 2)

Tilehurst, Woodley, Mortimer, Shinfield, Bracknell, Spencers Wood, Coley Park, Reading, West Reading, Wokingham, Burghfield Common, Newbury, Pangbourne, High Wycombe, Oare, Lower Earley, Haslemere, Burghfield

THE SALMON'S TALE (Tour 3)

Swindon, Haydon Wick, Stratton St Margaret, Covingham, Freshbrook, Highworth, Middleleaze, Croxley Green, Hemel Hempstead, Harpenden, Hatfield, St Albans, Broxbourne, Putney, Meryton, Wimbledon, Wandsworth, Bromley

2000

CARMEN

Greenwich, Bowness on Windermere, Clwyd, Hook (+overseas)

THE DREAMER (Tour 1)

Burghfield Common, Reading, Ascot, Swindon, Banbury, Henley, Northampton, Kingston, Oxford, Southampton, Wokingham, Wolverhampton, Willenhall, Birmingham, Walsall, Compton, Marlborough, Theale, Oxford, Shoreham

THE DREAMER (Tour 2)

Croydon, Wantage, Hampstead Norreys, Long Sutton, Swindon, Calne, Marlborough, Basingstoke, Lambourn, Bradfield, Chipping Norton, Stratton St Margaret, Southampton, Pewsey, Kintbury, Highworth, Devizes, Melksham, Aldbourne, Theale, Birmingham, Chester, Runcorn

2001

ROSE RAGE
Clwyd, Crawley, Leicester, Guildford, Manchester, Warwick, Huddersfield (+ overseas)

CARMEN & THE GONDOLIERS
Covent Garden Festival

LONE FLYER
Marlborough, Purton, Harwell, Northampton, Bicester, Highworth, Cricklade, Lambourn, Stratton, Maidenhead, Monxton, Testbourne, Cumnor, Shalbourne, Longworth, Witney, Hampstead Norreys, Calne, West Bromwich, Enham Alamein, Shrivenham, Abingdon, Kintbury, Wallingford, Croydon

WITCH
Calne, Pangbourne, Bucklebury, Middle Park, Highworth, Longworth, Shrivenham, Shalbourne, Wimbledon, Retford, Guildford, Wycombe, Theale, Hook, Hampstead Norreys, Pewsey, Langford, Wootton Bassett, Aldbourne, Monxton, Purton, Lambourn, Whitchurch, Kingsclere, Sevenoaks, Preston Brook, Ecclestone, Croydon

2002

ROSE RAGE
Oxford (+ overseas)

DANCING AT LUGHNASA
Greenwich

I DREAMT I DWELT IN MARBLE HALLS (Tour 1)
Calne, Highworth, Wootton Bassett, Horningsham, Dilton Marsh, Isle of Man, Hermitage, Shalbourne, Whitchurch, Marlborough, Pangbourne, Lambourn, Hungerford, Longworth, Hampstead Norreys, Kintbury, Wimbledon, Winchester, Abingdon, Beenham

I DREAMT I DWELT IN MARBLE HALLS (Tour 2)
Guildford, Old Jordan's Village, Thornborough, Claydon, Basingstoke, Ramsbury, Maidenhead, Wigmore,

Trowbridge, Aldbourne, Wimbledon, Warwick,
Shrivenham, Purton, Mere, Bucklebury, Reading, Pewsey,
Wigmore, London (Tricycle), Bristol, Poole

BETH THE BIN LADY

Compton, Newbury, Bradfield, Tilehurst, Wokingham,
Reading, Shaw-cum-Donnington, Abingdon, Burghfield,
Tilehurst, Swindon,

2003

A MIDSUMMER NIGHT'S DREAM

Bromley, Cambridge, Salford Quays, Guildford,
Richmond, Oxford, Newcastle (+ overseas)

GIGOLO (Tour 1)

Calne, Highworth, Hampstead Norreys, Hungerford,
Hawkesbury Upton, Winchester, Reading, Marlborough,
Hermitage, Winsley, Wimbledon, Birmingham, Leicester,
Shalbourne, Bucklebury, Dilton Marsh, Maidenhead,
Northleach, Poole, Beenham, Mere, Shrivenham,
Aldermaston, Bradfield, Wootton Bassett

GIGOLO (Tour 2)

Newbury, Atherstone, Guildford, Tiverton, Honiton,
Brighton, Trowbridge, New Milton, Bedworth, Stoke
Poges, Bath, Newark, Ollerton, Mansfield, Goostrey,
Plumley, Morehampstead, Kingsbridge, Okehampton,
Cirencester, Pewsey, Aldbourne, Stafford, Longworth,
Fringford, Sibford, Chippenham

2004

SWEENEY TODD

Bath, Liverpool, Huddersfield, Exeter, Guildford, Salford
Quays

MR & MRS SCHULTZ

Calne, Marlborough, Winchester, Highworth, Wootton
Bassett, Hawkesbury, Ramsbury, Trowbridge, Shalbourne,
Wolverhampton, Dudley, Hermitage, Northleach,

Shrivenham, Hampstead Norreys, Hungerford, Brimpton, Chippenham, Aldermaston

PINAFORE SWING

Richmond, Warwick, York, Portsmouth, Liverpool, Ipswich

THE COMEDIAN (Tour 1)

Calne, Hungerford, Aldermaston, Marlborough, Wootton Bassett, Chippenham, Lambourn, Brimpton, Hermitage, Pangbourne, Shrivenham, Pewsey, Longworth, Winchester, Northleach

2005

THE WINTER'S TALE (Tour 1)

Malvern, Guildford, Salford Quays, Liverpool, Oxford, Richmond, Newcastle (+ overseas)

THE WINTER'S TALE (Tour 2)

Swindon, Glasgow, Portsmouth, Cambridge, Canterbury, Aberystwyth (+ overseas)

THE COMEDIAN (Tour 2)

Tipton, Wolverhampton, Newark, Walsall, Eccleston, Plumley, Ramsbury, Amersham, Guildford, Uffington, Corsham, Mere, Wimbledon, Coleshill, Shalbourne, Trowbridge, Beenham

THE GARDEN OF LLANGOED

Abingdon, Wootton Bassett, Harlech, Bangor, Hampstead Norreys, Calne, Ilfracombe, Trowbridge, Malmesbury, Pewsey, Lambourn, Hungerford, Shrivenham, Taunton

WEST END TRANSFERS

1982

*This Thing Called Love_* – Duchess Theatre

1983

Snoopy – Duchess Theatre

2001

Rose Rage – Theatre Royal Haymarket

2003

A Midsummer Night's Dream – Comedy Theatre

2004

Sweeney Todd – Trafalgar Studios/ New Ambassadors Theatre

BROADWAY TRANSFER

2005

Sweeney Todd – Eugene O'Neill Theatre

Index